Gospel Joy

Pope Francis and the New Evangelization

Gospel Joy

Pope Francis and the New Evangelization

Dennis J. Billy, C.Ss.R.

New City Press
of the Focolare
Hyde Park, New York

Published in the United States by New City Press
202 Comforter Blvd., Hyde Park, NY 12538
www.newcitypress.com
© 2014 Dennis J. Billy

Cover design by Leandro De Leon

Cover Photo Courtesy of L'Osservatore Romano. Photo was taken when Pope Francis visited the slum area of Varginha, Brazil in July, 2013, used with Permission.

Bible citations unless otherwise noted are from the *New Revised Standard Version Bible*, copyright 1989, Division of Christian Education of the National Council of the Churches of Christ in the United States of America.

A catalog record is available from the Library of Congress.
ISBN: 978-1-56548-566-2

Contents

Introduction: The Joy of the Gospel 9

1: Changing Focus 13
    A Firm Foundation 14
    Gospel Living 16
    The Smell of the Sheep 19
    A Transforming Presence 22
    Conclusion 24
    Reflection Questions 26

2: Today's Challenges 27
    Present Challenges 29
    Present Temptations 31
    Saying "Yes" to God 34
    Living in the Spirit 37
    Conclusion 39
    Reflection Questions 41

3: The New Evangelization 43
    The Whole Church Proclaims 44
    Preaching the Word 49
    Understanding the Kerygma 54
    Conclusion 56
    Reflection Questions 58

4: Life in Communion 59
    Reaching Society 60
    Loving the Poor 63
    Dialogue for Peace 68
    Conclusion 72
    Reflection Questions 74

Conclusion: A Work of the Spirit 75
    Filled with the Spirit 76
    Turning to Mary 79

Notes 83

In fond memory of
José A. Serrano, II (1973–2013),
a disciple of Christ
and seminarian at
St. Charles Borromeo Seminary,
Wynnewood, Pennsylvania,
who embodied in his life
the Joy of the Gospel.

Go, therefore, and make disciples of all nations,
baptizing them in the name of the Father,
and of the Son, and of the Holy Spirit.

                                        Matthew 28:19

Introduction

The Joy of the Gospel

On March 13, 2013, when Cardinal Archbishop Jorge Mario Bergoglio of Buenos Aires (b. 1936) was elected Bishop of Rome, he took the name "Francis." The first pope from the Americas and the first Jesuit in that position, he has focused from the outset on the need within the Church for renewal at every level, the universal and local. A key element of his vision for renewal is the work of the new evangelization. On November 24, 2013, less than a year after his election, he promulgated *The Joy of the Gospel* (*Evangelii Gaudium*),[1] his apostolic exhortation on the proclamation of the gospel in today's world.

This book examines the central elements of Francis' vision of the Church as it sets out to preach the gospel to people of every nation and every walk of life. In four chapters, it examines the heart of his message and the focus of his vision for the future of Catholicism, Christianity, and the world. Central to that vision is his call to continue the new evangelization begun by

Pope St. John Paul II and embraced by his successor, Pope Benedict XVI. Pope St. John Paul II, especially in his early years, focused on the Communist threat in Eastern Europe and Benedict responded primarily to the challenges of secularization in the West. During the early part of his pontificate, however, Francis has focused on the world's poor and marginalized. Pope St. John Paul II, we might say, was an actor on the world's stage; Benedict XVI was the world's teacher; Pope Francis has become the world's pastor. Taking the reins of the papacy, he has turned it toward a living encounter with the tender and merciful God. Assuming the mantle of his predecessors with zeal and missionary abandon, he has added to their legacy his own distinct style and method, which focuses on a personal encounter with Jesus Christ and a call for peace and social justice.

These emphases come from his own rich life experience as a "missionary disciple" and emphasize his deep love for Jesus, Mary his mother, and the Church. A faithful, steadfast adherent of the Magisterium, Francis emphasizes the Church's love and tenderness for the world and all its people. Although he recognizes that evil always must be confronted and recognized for what it is, he also believes that it can be overcome only when humanity joyfully embraces the crucified, risen, and glorified Lord. For Francis, the revolutionary appeal of the gospel comes from the conviction that Jesus Christ has conquered sin and death and that the promise of plentiful redemption and fullness of life extends to everyone. This hope of our human transformation provides the underlying evangelical impulse for Jesus' followers to "make disciples of all nations" (Mt 28:19).

"Jesus Christ truly lives" (EG 275). This simple proclamation lies behind every dimension of Francis' outlook toward the new evangelization. For him, this statement represents not a mere myth concerning a universal truth about human existence, but an affirmation of faith in what happened to Jesus Christ after his passion and death on a cross. The narrative of Christ's paschal mystery is not merely a nice story that conveys some vague truth of humanity's existential awareness, but an actual reality. It points to the RISEN LORD who on Easter morning conquered death and at this moment lives in a transformed, glorified existence at the right hand of the Father.

This single proclamation — "Jesus lives" — offers hope to countless millions and points the way to the world's final transformation. Pope Francis believes we are called to happiness, both in this life and in the world to come. The Good News of Jesus' resurrection from the dead, he thinks, bestows hope that we too will conquer death and one day experience the fullness of the beatific happiness for which we were made. Ever since the beginning, the Church has proclaimed this message and will continue to do so, despite the challenges ahead or the rejection it may face. The Church receives the strength to do so from the presence of Christ's Spirit. This living presence fortifies the faithful and enkindles in them a burning love for the Risen Lord. The kingdom of God is both within them and in their midst (Lk 17:21). Their power to convince comes from the love they manifest underlying evangelical impulse for Jesus' followers to "make disciples of all nations" (Mt 28:19).

"Jesus Christ truly lives" (EG 275). This simple proclamation lies behind every dimension of Francis' outlook toward the new evangelization. For him, this statement represents not a mere myth concerning a universal truth about human existence, but an affirmation of faith in what happened to Jesus Christ after his passion and death on a cross. The narrative of Christ's paschal mystery is not merely a nice story that conveys some vague truth of humanity's existential awareness, but an actual reality. It points to the RISEN LORD who on Easter morning conquered death and at this moment lives in a transformed, glorified existence at the right hand of the Father.

This single proclamation—"Jesus lives"—offers hope to countless millions and points the way to the world's final transformation. Pope Francis believes we are called to happiness, both in this life and in the world to come. The Good News of Jesus' resurrection from the dead, he thinks, bestows hope that we too will conquer death and one day experience the fullness of the beatific happiness for which we were made. Ever since the beginning, the Church has proclaimed this message and will continue to do so, despite the challenges ahead or the rejection it may face. The Church receives the strength to do so from the presence of Christ's Spirit. This living presence fortifies the faithful and enkindles in them a burning love for the Risen Lord. The kingdom of God is both within them and in their midst (Lk 17:21). Their power to convince comes from the love they manifest in their lives, a love that comes not from them, but from the Spirit of Christ living within them.

This book cannot capture the entirety of Francis' vision of the Church striving to proclaim the gospel in today's world, but it seeks to touch upon the main contours of the pope's message, which focuses on God's tenderness, love, and compassion for all human beings. Pope Francis proclaims a gospel of joy as well as a gospel of mercy, one in which the shepherds must be close to their people, love them, and carry about them "the smell of their sheep."[2]

1

Changing Focus

I prefer a Church bruised, hurting and dirty because it has been out on the streets, rather than a Church unhealthy from being confined and from clinging to its own security. I want no Church concerned with being at the center and which then ends by being caught up in a web of obsessions and procedures. If something should rightly disturb us and trouble our consciences, it is that so many of our brothers and sisters are living without the strength, light and consolation born of friendship with Jesus Christ, without a community of faith to support them, without meaning and a goal in life. More than by fear of going astray, I hope that we will be moved by the fear of remaining shut up within structures, within rules which make us harsh judges, within habits which make us feel safe, while at our door people are starving and Jesus does not tire of saying to us: "Give them something to eat" (Mk 6:37).

Evangelii Gaudium, 49

*T*hese words exemplify the change of focus that Pope Francis, in the opening months of his pontificate, has brought to the forefront of Catholic consciousness, a change that will inspire us for years to come. He does not present impossible goals that would only weary us, empty hopes that would only disappoint and weaken our resolve, added burdens that would distract us from our purpose, but a vision of the Church that asks each and every one of us take stock of the essentials of our faith and focus on what truly matters.

Pope Francis calls us back to the basics. Like Francis of Assisi, whose name he bears, he asks us to embrace the simple message of God's deep, passionate love for every human person, especially the poor and neglected. Jesus Christ embodies this love; all who call themselves Christians are his friends. Whatever we think and say and do must flow from this friendship. If it does not, our faith becomes a mockery, something other than the very faith of Jesus Christ.

A Firm Foundation

When Jesus cautioned his followers to build their houses on rock lest they be swept away by rain, wind, and flood, he was not giving architectural advice. The parable is about our spiritual life. If we don't get the basics straight, we risk losing everything. Pope Francis also challenges us to take careful stock of our situation, to step back and take a good, hard look at ourselves so we can see things more clearly and set our priorities straight. He reminds us that some aspects of faith are more important; it would be a distortion to assign greater significance to lesser truths (important as they may be). He advises us to build our lives on a firm foundation. Jesus puts it this way:

> ""Everyone then who hears these words of mine and acts on them will be like a wise man who built his house on rock. The rain fell, the floods came, and the winds blew and beat on that house, but it did not fall, because it had been founded on rock. And everyone who hears these words of mine and does not act on them will be like a foolish man who built his house on sand. The rain fell, and the floods came, and the winds blew and beat against that house, and it fell—and great was its fall!"
> (Mt 7:24–29)[3]

If the foundation is solid, the house will stand; if weak, it will fall. Jesus does not want us to be fools, but wise disciples. Following him is the one thing necessary. All else is secondary. If we build on him, we will experience the fullness of life. If we choose to go it alone, we must live with the consequences.

Francis asks us to avoid being distracted by secondary issues that, although worthwhile, can cause us to lose sight of life's true purpose. Christianity is not a moral cause, but a way of life centered on the person of Jesus Christ. Unless seen from the perspective of this fundamental truth of the Christian faith, all the other aspects make no sensible pattern. Francis wants us to view things properly, not focusing on smaller details but on the complete picture.

The pope's advice reflects what is often called the "hierarchy of truths" (EG 36). The Church's doctrines are not all equal; some are fundamental and therefore carry more weight than others. The dogma of the Trinity, which stands at the top of this hierarchy, is much more important than the dogma of the Virgin Birth. Similarly, even though both are solemnly defined dogmas of the faith, the Incarnation occupies a higher place in the hierarchy than does the Immaculate Conception. Because the different aspects of Catholic teaching carry different values, we can focus on what really matters because we believe and know why they matter. Although the truths may compete for our attention, we would know which of them deserves special reverence.

Gospel Living

This hierarchy of truths, the pope maintains, applies not only to doctrinal teachings but also to the Church's moral assertions (EG 37). Jesus himself has no difficulty distinguishing between the essential and the non-essential: "In everything do to others as you would have them do to you; for this is the law and the prophets" (Mt 7:12). When asked to name the greatest commandment, he replies: "'You shall love the Lord your God with all your heart, and with all your soul, and with all your mind.' This is the greatest and first commandment. And a second is like it: 'You shall love your neighbor as yourself.' On these two commandments hang all the law and the prophets" (Mt 22:37–40). Concerning the theological virtues, the apostle Paul says something similar: "For the whole law is summed up in a single commandment, 'You shall love your neighbor as yourself'" (Gal 5:14). Elsewhere, he writes: "And now faith, hope, and love abide, these three; and the greatest of these is love" (1 Cor 13:13). No matter how Christian love might be named — charity, a*gape*, the "Golden Rule" — it is synonymous with the gospel message. It deserves a place of reverence in the Church's teaching and a prominent place in our hearts.

Pope Francis puts it this way: "Works of love directed to one's neighbor are the most perfect external expression of the interior grace of the Spirit" (EG 37). Speaking of the effects of love, he points to St. Thomas' teaching that mercy is the greatest of the virtues not only because the others revolve around it, but also because it makes up for their deficiencies.[4] In the pope's mind, mercy lies at the heart of the gospel and is the *sine qua non* of Christian living (EG 37). We see how thoroughly mercy permeated Jesus' thoughts and actions in his encounter with the woman caught in adultery (Jn 8:1–11), his curing the paralytic lowered through a roof on a stretcher (Lk 5:17–32), his parable of the prodigal son (Lk 15:1–32), and his words of forgiveness from the cross (Lk 23:34).

Those who have received mercy are called to extend it to others. Also, the pope says, the precepts of God's law should be applied with moderation (EG 38, 43). They should be considered not as threats but as guideposts that indicate the way of the Lord Jesus. The moral law lays out the way of discipleship and represents true gospel living. We embrace it not as an end but to give witness to the truth and to follow in the footsteps of Jesus, Our Lord, who said, "If any want to become my followers, let them deny themselves and take up their cross daily and follow me" (Lk 9:23).

What is Francis getting at? Christianity, he insists, is more than a list of rules and regulations. Despite the commandments' importance for Christian life, only one thing truly matters: our relationship with Jesus Christ (EG 3). If Christians focus so much on the Church's moral teachings (even basic teachings regarding the dignity of the human person and the sanctity of all human life), they may miss the joy that flows from our friendship with Christ. Francis worries that despite our good intentions, we may have misplaced our priorities. When we do so, Christianity becomes a burden rather a joy and our lives seem like an endless "Lent without Easter" (EG 6). Practicing our faith may be reduced to a list of "dos and don'ts" rather than a heartfelt living-out of our love for God manifested in observing what is good and avoiding what is evil. We are called to be joyful missionary disciples of an evangelizing community, not dour proponents of an exacting and unforgiving ecclesial institution. Francis asks us not only to change direction but also to change our hearts. If we concentrate our energies on our relationship with Jesus, everything else will fall in place.

The Smell of the Sheep

Pope Francis has said, memorably, that the evangelizing community must take on the "smell of the sheep" (EG 24). These words apply not merely to those with leadership roles such as bishops, priests, and religious, but to all members of the believing community. Jesus' followers are called to get their hands dirty, to contact the lost or marginalized. They must welcome the stranger, comfort the sick, feed the hungry, and visit those in prison (Mt 25:31–46). Jesus calls them to seek the impoverished and the needy, treating them with the dignity they deserve. They do so because Jesus did this. This was his *modus operandi*, his way of acting. He himself said, "'Truly I tell you, just as you did it to one of the least of these who are members of my family, you did it to me'" (Mt 25: 40).

The entire gospel message is based on the premise that God seeks those who have strayed from his love. What is Christianity all about? This: God loved us so much he entered our world (in the Incarnation), gave himself to us completely to the point of dying for us (in his passion and death), to become nourishment for us (in the Eucharist) and a source of hope (in his Resurrection). Christianity must not be limited to our search for God; it is above all God's search for us. God pursues us like a shepherd seeking his lost sheep (Lk 15:1–7) or the woman who sweeps her house looking for a lost coin (Lk 15:8–10) or the father who rushes out of his house to greet his returning prodigal son (Lk 15:20). To cite Francis Thompson's poem, God is like a "hound of heaven" who pursues us "down the nights and down the days…down the arches of the years…down the labyrinthine ways."[5] He does this for no other reason than that he loves us. "God is love" (1 Jn 4:8), John's gospel says, a love that is self-diffusive, that can hardly contain itself. God pursues us because he is madly in love with us. He is "Iddio Pazzo," as St. Alphonsus de Liguori was fond of saying, "a crazy God," whose extreme love for us is revealed in what, humanly speaking, seem extreme measures.[6]

Taking on the "smell of the sheep" recalls an early Christian depiction of Jesus as the Good Shepherd returning to his flock carrying a lost lamb over his shoulders. Based on Jesus' parable of the lost sheep (Lk 15:1–7) and his description of himself as the good shepherd who lays down his life for his sheep (Jn 10:11), the image illustrates the lengths to which God secures our safety and well-being. Pope Francis notes that Christians are not merely to ponder love, but to put it into action. It is the love of the Word-made-flesh who "lived among us" (Jn 1: 14). It speaks of the love of a God who entered human life in the darkness of his mother's womb and who left it in the darkness of an empty tomb. It is a reminder that from his birth in Bethlehem to his death in Jerusalem, Jesus' earthly life was marked by a closeness to the people unprecedented in the priestly or prophetic tradition. Out of love he spoke with authority, proclaimed the imminent arrival of God's reign, demonstrating it through astonishing teachings, powerful works of healing, and dramatic expressions of compassion and forgiveness.

Francis' message is simple: Since Christ took on the smell of the sheep, so must we. He warns Christians against letting their faith become an armchair religion, as if they could live the gospel from afar, without getting involved in any of the grimy details of life, escaping its daily challenges. This warning applies to all of Christ's followers, especially to its leaders. Pope Francis cites the three major temptations the Church today must resist: that it be run like a business, that it be treated like an ideology, and that it foster clericalism and careerism.[7] He acknowledges the Church's need to clean house, to renew its structures at every level, beginning with the papacy and the curia and extending to every level of its organization (EG 27–33). Jesus said, "[W]hoever wishes to be great among you must be your servant, and whoever wishes to be first among you must be your slave; just as the Son of Man came not to be served but to serve, and to give his life a ransom for many" (Mt 20:26–28). Recognizing that "mere administration can no longer be enough," Pope Francis calls us to be "permanently in a state of mission" (EG 23).

Church institutions must serve the people of God—not vice versa. They exist not to perpetuate themselves, but to benefit God's people. The Church is not a bureaucracy, but a family. When its leaders lose sight of their purpose, when they forget what they are about and why they hold the positions they do, it is time for change. "The wind blows where it chooses" (Jn 3:8); the Spirit moves in God's good time. Pope Francis knows that the Spirit has always been with the Church and will never abandon God's family. He recognizes that the Church is called to continual conversion, a call in every generation. The word "conversion" (or *metanoia* in the Greek) means turning around, having a fundamental change of heart. This call, which lies at the heart of the pope's message, is meant for all who have ears to hear. To carry out its mission, the Church must look at its structures, examine its motives, and make adjustments for the good of God's people. Only a Church renewed — on all its levels — can help bring about a renewal of hearts in the world today.

A Transforming Presence

Renewing the human heart is a work of God. We share in this work by cooperating with it. Before his return to the Father, the Risen Lord gave the apostles a missionary mandate: "Go therefore and make disciples of all nations, baptizing them in the name of the Father and of the Son and of the Holy Spirit, and teaching them to obey everything that I have commanded you" (Mt 28:19–20). This mission touches the heart of the Church's existence and underscores its intimate relationship to Christ who, as head of the body, the Church, has promised to remain with us always "to the end of the age" (Mt 28:20).

The Church, Francis tells us, goes forth on its apostolic activity to convert and transform the world. Its transforming presence announces God's kingdom and makes it a reality through preaching (*kerygma*), fellowship *(koinonia)*, service (*diakonia*), and celebration of the sacraments (*liturgia*), all of which are actions of Christ that herald the new creation. If the Church is to transform the world, Pope Francis reminds us, its members must be converted to Christ. Our message must flow from the heart of the gospel, which has taken root in our souls.

This mission, the pope tells us, must take a human shape and so must be continually reformulated in language and expressions that are meaningful to those who hear it. He asks us to recognize the difference between the gospel itself and the forms used to express it (EG 41). As at Pentecost the disciples proclaimed the Good News in different languages, bringing about the conversion of many (Acts 2:1–13), so are we called to discover new ways to touch the hearts of those we encounter. Our mission therefore requires ongoing discernment concerning the way we preach, teach, serve, and celebrate. Also remember that our mission, which is both *ad intra* and *ad extra,* involves reaching in and reaching out. We ourselves must be evangelized to carry out our evangelizing mission.

In all of this, Pope Francis maintains, the Church remains a "mother with an open heart" (EG 46). She always leaves her door open and extends an invitation to everyone to share in her life: "Everyone can share in some way in the life of the Church; everyone can be part of the community" (EG 47). He points out that "the doors of the sacraments [must] not be closed for simply any reason" (EG 47). The Eucharist, in particular, should not be a "prize for the perfect," but "powerful medicine and nourishment for the weak" (EG 47). "[T]he confessional," moreover, "must not be a torture chamber but rather an encounter with the Lord's mercy which spurs us on to do our best" (EG 44). Also, "there is an inseparable bond between our faith and the poor" (EG 48). The Church, therefore, must go out to everyone without exception and offer them the life of Jesus Christ. The gospels indicate clearly that we should seek "not so much our friends and wealthy neighbors, but above all the poor and the sick, those who are usually despised and overlooked, 'those who cannot repay you'" (EG 48).

Conclusion

Pope Francis affirms the Church's missionary mandate to go forth and make disciples of all nations, a mandate that applies not only to clergy and religious but to every member of the faithful. As individual believers and as members of a community, evangelization requires us to abandon our complacency, to spread the Good News of Jesus Christ boldly, creatively.

To succeed in the new evangelization, we must first be evangelized ourselves. We cannot give what we ourselves do not have. Being "sacramentalized" does not mean that we have been "evangelized"; many practicing Catholics have yet to experience the joy of Christ's friendship.[8] The Church's missionary transformation must begin in our hearts and work its way outwards. It requires us to examine and rethink "the goals, structures, style and method of evangelization" (EG 33) at every level, from the Vatican to local dioceses to parishes to families, and to individuals.

Our motives must be completely transparent; we must take special care to practice what we preach. Our evangelizing efforts should energize our ordinary pastoral ministry to contact those who no longer practice their faith, even those who may have never heard the gospel message or even may have rejected it (EG 15).

The joy of the gospel is synonymous with friendship with Christ. This intimate personal relationship, which lies at the heart of the faith, changes our lives in untold ways. It is our primary means for making new disciples. When Christ's love burns in our hearts, the power of the Lord's Spirit is unleashed in our lives and wonderful things happen. Transformed by Jesus' compassion, mercy, and love we feel compelled to share it with others. Such sharing lies at the heart of our missionary mandate. When we share our experience of Christ's friendship we make disciples just as Jesus did with his earliest followers: "Come to me, all you that are weary and are carrying heavy burdens, and I will give you rest. Take my yoke upon you, and learn from me; for I am gentle and humble in heart, and you will find rest for your souls. For my yoke is easy, and my burden is light" (Mt 11:28–30). Pope Francis understands that the joy of the gospel comes from resting in the friendship and love of Christ. From this perspective, the message we proclaim is welcomed with relief because it promises great joy.

Reflection Questions

* When have you experienced the joy of Christ's friendship? How was this friendship important to you? What other forces in your life are important?

* What does Christ ask of you? How does he challenge you? How might you change focus? In what ways do you need renewal?

* In what areas does the Church need renewal? How can you participate in this work of renewal?

* What value does the work of making disciples have for you? How can you participate in the new evangelization? How can you help make disciples in your daily life?

2

Today's Challenges

The Christian ideal will always be a summons to overcome suspicion, habitual mistrust, fear of losing our privacy, all the defensive attitudes which today's world imposes on us. Many try to escape from others and take refuge in the comfort of their privacy or in a small circle of close friends, renouncing the realism of the social aspect of the gospel. For just as some people want a purely spiritual Christ, without flesh and without the cross, they also want their interpersonal relationships provided by sophisticated equipment, by screens and systems which can be turned on and off on command. Meanwhile, the gospel tells us constantly to risk a face-to-face encounter with others, with their physical presence which challenges us, with their pain and their pleas, with their joy which infects us in our close and continuous interaction. True faith in the incarnate Son of God is inseparable from self-giving, from membership in the community, from service, from reconciliation with others. The Son of God, by becoming flesh, summoned us to the revolution of tenderness.

Evangelii Gaudium, 88

The new evangelization challenges us to be active participants in a "revolution of tenderness" which, rooted in God's face-to-face encounter with us in the person of Jesus Christ, abhors violence and seeks a radical change in outlook through peaceful means. In taking on human nature in solidarity with us, God has taken on our point of view and has experienced the trials and challenges that fill our lives. By living among us, he knows intimately the temptations and suffering of being immersed in a broken world. Jesus, the Word-made-flesh, calls us to be in the world but not of it, to embrace the world, to be a leaven for it, and ultimately bring about its transformation. He wants us to be missionary disciples who, like him, follow the path of selfless giving to draw others into the sphere of divine love. We do so by fostering personal friendships through face-to-face encounters, sharing with these friends the joy of the gospel. Pope Francis refers to the "revolution of tenderness," by which we set aside the values of the world and adopt those Jesus has described in the Sermon on the Mount, in which we find the Beatitudes and even the Golden Rule (Mt 5–7).

Easier said than done. The pope understands the challenges that missionary disciples are facing at the dawn of the twenty-first century. In keeping with his formation in Ignatian spirituality, he asks us to be ever watchful of the "signs of the times" and to discern between the spirit of good and the spirit of evil. He recognizes the dehumanizing tendencies that block Christ being borne to others through evangelization (EG 51). He also believes this moment in history, marked by great technological advancement as well as growing fear and desperation, is a turning point in human experience. It is a conflict that has unsettling results: "The joy of living frequently fades, lack of respect for others and violence is on the rise, and inequality is increasingly evident. It is a struggle to live and, often, to live with precious little dignity" (EG 52). Contemporary challenges demand creative approaches which may have unorthodox or unprecedented solutions.

Present Challenges

A middle school science teacher once engaged her students in studying aerodynamics by giving them a challenge. She gave them fifteen minutes to construct a paper airplane that would travel the greatest distance, using only a single sheet of paper. Her students displayed great creativity within the allotted time and came up with a variety of designs they hoped would outdo their classmates. The winner turned out to be Jeffrey, a young boy known for unconventional behavior. He approached the line slowly, hiding something behind his back. To his teacher's and classmates' surprise he produced a plain sheet of paper. After the snickering died down, he crumpled the paper into a ball and heaved it as hard as he could. No one could match his distance. Jeffrey interpreted the challenge in a unique way and had the courage to act upon his vision.[9]

In a similar way, our journey of faith will include inevitable challenges, but we can develop our own creative responses. Jesus' disciples faced enormous challenges as they began their journeys; we should not expect otherwise. The apostle Paul writes, "We are afflicted in every way, but not crushed; perplexed, but not driven to despair; persecuted, but not forsaken; struck down, but not destroyed" (2 Cor 4:8–9). The pope asks us not to lose heart, to be creative and courageous in following the Lord, who promises not to abandon us. We need to look beyond ourselves and turn to the Lord of impossible things. St. Paul says, "I can do all things through him who strengthens me" (Phil 4:13). As we make our way through this troubled world, the pope counsels us to be "nourished by the light and strength of the Holy Spirit," and suggests how to do so (EG 50).

Pope Francis begins by focusing on the "economy of exclusion" (EG 53). He is not an economist and does not prefer one particular economic system above others; he acknowledges the Church's teaching on private property and the universal destination of goods. He is concerned about the dangerous effects of unbridled capitalism, especially the tendency in it to view human beings as consumer goods, promoting a selfish lifestyle and reinforcing indifference to the poor and marginalized. He also criticizes the "new idolatry of money" and its promotion of "the dictatorship of an impersonal economy lacking a truly human purpose" (EG 55). Such a system in which money rules rather than serves, he claims, devalues ethics, and promotes an atmosphere of self-interest in which the plight of others is disregarded (EG 57–58).

A society with such a limited worldview is marked not only by the division between "haves" and "have-nots," but also by a culture of violence (EG 59). Such a perspective promotes a superficial understanding of the human person, encourages judgment solely by appearances, relishes subjective truth, advances relativism, unleashes secularization, and ultimately contributes to unbridled individualism and the breakdown of the family (EG 61–67). Francis warns these challenges affect nearly everyone and make inculturating the faith more difficult, especially in urban centers, where people feel increasingly isolated from one another and are beset by dehumanizing influences (EG 68–75). What C. S. Lewis calls the "abolition of man"—the tendency to treat people as objects rather than subjects—becomes easy. When that happens, people become raw material to be manipulated, used, and ultimately discarded when they no longer seem useful.[10] No one would be dehumanized in this way, but the poor and marginalized are often treated like this.

Present Temptations

Pope Francis realizes these challenges affect those who provide pastoral care in the Church. Ministry is paradoxical: God uses weak human beings to carry out his work. Paul himself writes, "But we have this treasure in clay jars, so that it may be made clear that this extraordinary power belongs to God and does not come from us" (2 Cor 4:7). Elsewhere he writes: "Therefore I am content with weaknesses, insults, hardships, persecutions, and calamities for the sake of Christ; for whenever I am weak, then I am strong" (2 Cor 12:10). Francis enumerates the temptations and hardships that can prevent us from embracing our call to be "missionary disciples." He understands that "all of us are in some way affected by the present globalized culture which, while offering us values and new possibilities, can also limit, condition and ultimately harm us" (EG 77).

What might these temptations be? First, a "heightened individualism" can generate "an inordinate concern for...personal freedom and relaxation" that leads to work becoming a mere appendage to life, as if it were not an integral part of Christian identity (EG 78). The media and certain learned circles convey "a marked skepticism with regard to the Church's message, along with a certain cynicism" (EG 79). Our inner conflict can lead to an "inferiority complex" that softens Christian values and conceals Christian identity and convictions (EG 79). The resulting "vicious circle" makes us unhappy about our identity and our behavior (EG 79). Such mistrust of the Church and our own Christian identity leads to a "practical relativism." Although we may profess our beliefs publicly, our "missionary enthusiasm" weakens, causing us to act "as if God did not exist" (EG 80). We walk a tightrope between countervailing rational and irrational forces, sometimes losing our balance.

This "practical relativism" leads to other problems. We obsess about protecting our free time and consider evangelization as "a dangerous poison rather than a joyful response to God's love which summons us to mission and makes us fulfilled and productive" (EG 81). "Spiritual sloth" makes us feel discouraged and weary: "Far from a content and happy tiredness, this is a tense, burdensome, dissatisfying and, in the end, unbearable fatigue" (EG 82). Because our culture prizes immediate satisfaction, we balk at "anything that smacks of disagreement, possible failure, criticism, the cross" (EG 82). The biggest threat is "the gray pragmatism of the daily life of the Church, in which all appears to proceed normally, while in reality faith is wearing down and degenerating into small-mindedness" (EG 83). This petty "tomb psychology … slowly transforms Christians into mummies in a museum," without hope and infected by a latent melancholy that blots out our gospel joy (EG 83).

We must cast off such negativity, which turns us into the "living dead." Jesus himself says that ours is a God of the living, and not of the dead (see Mk12: 27). Francis exhorts us to reject the spiritual pessimism and worldliness that can easily infect our minds and hearts. He encourages us to resist "a defeatism which turns us into querulous and disillusioned pessimists, 'sourpusses'" (EG 85). No one likes a grumpy disciple. The pope also bids us to cooperate with one another and to refuse the spiritual "desertification" that can affect the public square, the workplace, the family, the human heart, every area of life. In this spiritual desert, he sees a unique opportunity to discover the deep spiritual thirst and hunger of the heart by which we can "rediscover the value of what is essential for living" (EG 86). With the eyes of faith "we can see the light which the Holy Spirit always radiates in the midst of darkness" (EG 84). The Lord offered himself "as a source of living water"; "we are called to be living sources of water from which others can drink" (EG 86).

Saying "Yes" to God

Christian life can be described as a movement away from the disordered attachments of the world ("detachment") and toward the things of God or "life in the Spirit" ("union"). St. Paul puts it this way: "For those who live according to the flesh set their minds on the things of the flesh, but those who live according to the Spirit set their minds on the things of the Spirit" (Rom 8:5). Reflecting this important principle of the spiritual life, Pope Francis tells us that as missionary disciples we must say "no" to some things and "yes" to others.

Earlier in his message he says "no" to the economy of exclusion, the new idolatry of money, a financial system that rules rather than serves, and an inequality that spawns violence. He cites the challenges that make inculturating the faith in today's world difficult, challenges that affect every Christian. So we also must say "no" to selfishness, complacency, and the sterile pessimism that can make us ashamed of our faith, embrace a relativistic attitude toward life, and even turn us into practical atheists. Pope Francis calls for a "no" to the spiritual worldliness that divides our hearts that sets us against ourselves and others. Christianity is not a religion of "dos and don'ts." We say "no" to certain things not for the sake of saying "no," but because we have discovered a "pearl of great price" (Mt 13:46), which is the only thing that matters: our relationship with Jesus Christ.

The pope wants us to say "yes" to whatever will deepen our relationship with Christ. To do so, we must open our hearts in prayer, asking God to reveal himself to us. We must get down on our knees and ask for help in establishing a personal relationship with God. We must spend time in silent prayer seeking deep within our hearts the One all along seeking us. We must attend to the still, small voice within our hearts constantly whispering, "I love you. I love you. I love you." We must become one of the Lord Jesus' disciples and embrace the challenge of missionary spirituality. We must go forth and make disciples of those we encounter in our daily lives through the words we say, and the things we do. We must witness to Christ's love for us through selfless giving to everyone we meet, especially the poor and marginalized.

After saying "yes" to Christ by inviting him into our hearts and following him as missionary disciples, we must also say "yes" to his Spirit, who lights up our path and through holy promptings guides us. Saying "yes" to the Spirit means saying "yes" to relationships rooted in Christ, forged in love, and open to new life. We are called out of isolation and challenged "to overcome suspicion, habitual mistrust, fear of losing our privacy, all the defensive attitudes which today's world imposes on us" (EG 88). Rather than escaping into the comfort of a small circle of friends, turning ourselves inward and away from the social dimension of the gospel, we are called to face-to-face encounters by which we can carry to them Christ's invitation to plentiful and abundant life. If we allow God to live in our hearts and his Spirit to shape and polish us into images of divine love, we bear Christ to others. The apostle Paul describes what this entails:

> As God's chosen ones, holy and beloved, clothe yourselves with compassion, kindness, humility, meekness, and patience. Bear with one another and, if anyone has a complaint against another, forgive each other; just as the Lord has forgiven you, so you also must forgive. Above all, clothe yourselves with love, which binds everything together in perfect harmony. And let the peace of Christ rule in your hearts, to which you were called in the one body. And be thankful. Let the word of Christ dwell in you richly; teach and admonish one another in all wisdom; and with gratitude in your hearts sing psalms, hymns, and spiritual songs to God. And whatever you do, in word or deed, do everything in the name of the Lord Jesus, giving thanks to God the Father through him.
>
> Col 3:12–17

God shapes each of us into an *alter Christus* (another Christ) by entering into relationship with us and offering his friendship (Jn 15:15), which is marked by benevolence, reciprocity, and mutual indwelling.[11] Sirach says, "Faithful friends are a sturdy shelter" (Sir 6:14 NAB). True friends look out for one another and carry each other in their hearts. Being friends with Christ means he seeks our well-being and in return we seek to do his will. He dwells in our hearts and we dwell in his. As Paul eloquently attests:

"For through the law I died to the law, so that I might live to God. I have been crucified with Christ; and it is no longer I who live, but it is Christ who lives in me. And the life I now live in the flesh I live by faith in the Son of God, who loved me and gave himself for me" (Gal 2:19–21). To live in Christ means to die to sin and the works of the flesh, to be filled with his Spirit manifested by spiritual fruits: "love, joy, peace, patience, kindness, generosity, faithfulness, gentleness, and self-control" (Gal 5: 22–23). By these signs others will see we are followers of Christ. The more these fruits are manifested in our lives, the more closely are our hearts conformed to Christ, and Christ to ours.

Living in the Spirit

Disciples today face many challenges, both negative and positive. The negative ones come from the world's distractions and misdirected values that weigh us down and distract us from our goal, pulling us from our ultimate purpose in life. We become divided both within ourselves and in our relationship with others.

On the positive side, God challenges us to relinquish whatever prevents us from loving him and to cling to whatever deepens our love for him and our desire to live for others. The challenge of discipleship, its "cost," is a gradual process of conversion in which we loosen our hold onto our own lives and allow God's Spirit to take possession of us and move us along the way of holiness. Alphonsus de Liguori said that "the paradise of God is the human heart."[12] For Pope Francis, the joy of the gospel is simple: God wishes to live in our hearts. When we let God do so his Spirit dwells there, purging our imperfections and slowly divinizing us so that as free and faithful disciples we follow the way of the Lord Jesus. Being a disciple challenges us to allow our relationship with Christ to become so intimate we identify completely with him and our life becomes a continual dance, his Spirit who resides in our hearts directing and prompting us from within.

Before all else, being led by the Spirit means being committed to a life of prayer. When he was Archbishop of Buenos Aires, Jorge Mario Bergoglio wrote: "Prayer is talking and listening. There are moments of profound silence, adoration, waiting to see what will happen."[13] Prayer, he says, is the space in our lives we open up to God. We can do this: through petitions, meditation, reading Scripture, contemplation—to name a few. Since we are both individual and social by nature, it also follows that our prayer will reflect a balance between personal devotion and membership in Christ's body, the Church. "The spirit of the liturgical celebration," Archbishop Bergoglio maintained, "must be linked with the spiritual, with the encounter with God."[14] Prayer is our encounter with God; it is the air we breathe that helps us to live a life in the Spirit. We may not see the Spirit's presence in our lives if we have not sought the Lord in prayer. Any close relationship must be nurtured through spending time with each other. The same is true of our rapport with God. We nurture our relationship with him when we seek him in prayer with body, mind, and spirit. If we do not pray, we can never be on intimate terms with God. If we do not pray, we will not understand how to live a life led by the Spirit. We may know something about the Spirit, but we will never experience the Spirit working actively in our lives.

The Spirit's presence in our lives makes various gifts and fruits work in harmony to achieve a synergy within us. Aristotle observed that "The whole is greater than the sum of the parts."[15] Our "parts" operate in concert with one another, rarely in isolation. The Spirit's gifts and fruits do not call attention to themselves or even to the person upon whom they are bestowed. They exist to give God glory by transforming us more and more into his image and likeness. They may not always be active; the Spirit puts them to use as the need arises. Ultimately, gospel joy comes from our cooperation with God's free offer of abundant grace.

Conclusion

Disciples face many complex challenges: individualism, secularization, the idolatry of money, globalization, relativism, and practical atheism—to name but a few. Their inescapable influence fills our world. We may even feel overwhelmed by them. Pope Francis identifies these challenges, names them for what they are, and encourages us not to lose hope. Discipleship, he reminds us, demands courage and strength. Following Jesus means taking up the cross and walking in his footsteps. These challenges demand original thinking, that we look beyond the cross, fixing our eyes on the empty tomb and opening our hearts to the Spirit of the Risen Lord.

The earliest disciples knew what they would face. Jesus himself warned them: "If the world hates you, be aware that it hated me before it hated you... . . If they persecuted me, they will persecute you" (Jn 15:18, 20). At his command, his disciples traveled the world, took risks, and faced countless dangers with great courage These challenges did not discourage them because in the face of insurmountable odds the Spirit comforted them, strengthened their resolve, emboldened them, and confirmed them in their mission. Their love for God and the Spirit of the Lord moved these disciples to share that love with others.

Some of our challenges resemble those of the earliest disciples; others, products of our own day and age, demand new and untried responses. However they affect us—in ways large or small—Pope Francis encourages us to face them head-on with the same missionary zeal: "Challenges exist to be overcome! Let us be realists, but without losing our joy, our boldness and our hope-filled commitment. Let us not allow ourselves to be robbed of our missionary vigor!" (EG 109).

Reflection Questions

* What challenges do you face in your daily life? Where do they come from? How are you dealing with them? How do they hold you back or prevent you from following Jesus?

* Are you affected by any that Pope Francis mentions? Which affect you more than others? Which have worn you down? Which seem to diminish your joy and missionary vigor? What can you do to regain what you have lost?

* How do these challenges offer an opportunity for growth? With God all things are possible. How does knowing that help you?

3

The New Evangelization

> The Lord's missionary mandate includes a call to growth in faith: "Teach them to observe all that I have commanded you" (Mt 28:20). Hence the first proclamation also calls for ongoing formation and maturation. Evangelization aims at a process of growth which entails taking seriously each person and God's plan for his or her life. All of us need to grow in Christ. Evangelization should stimulate a desire for this growth, so that each of us can say wholeheartedly: "It is no longer I who live, but Christ who lives in me" (Gal 2:20).
>
> *Evangelii Gaudium*, 160

*T*he Church faces the challenge of working to develop the new evangelization. These efforts are "new" not because the original proclamation was weak and ineffective, but because the gospel message must be preached anew to every generation. This proclamation, must touch people's lives and speak to their hearts. Otherwise, the gospel can lose its vigor, become stale or irrelevant, and seem more like "No News" than the "Good News" it is.

Many Christians, ourselves included, may have been "sacramentalized" but not "evangelized." I know I was (and feel I still am!). Receiving the sacraments does not make us true disciples. They are not magical incantations, but living signs and concrete invitations that deepen our relationship with Christ so we can give witness to him in our lives. To put it another way, we are called both to evangelize and be evangelized. The encounter with Jesus Christ always leads to being sent to others by Jesus Christ. Pope Francis points out that the gospel is not a mummified artifact on display in a museum, but a vibrant, living reality that motivates our hearts and minds. Jesus' mandate to make disciples of all nations applies as much to us as it did to his earliest followers. We must not ignore our mission of proclaiming God's love; we must strive to find new ways of communicating this message. Jesus said, "No one puts new wine into old wineskins; otherwise, the wine will burst the skins, and the wine is lost, and so are the skins; but one puts new wine into fresh wineskins." (Mk 2:22). The wine of the gospel is forever new. Today, as always, we must present it so it meets people where they are, speaks to their present circumstances, and calls them to a change of heart.

The Whole Church Proclaims

The Church may be on a pilgrim journey, but sometimes it seems to be traveling at a snail's pace, on crutches and with one hand tied behind its back. It doesn't seem to use its most important asset: its people. The faithful seem detached, uninvolved in carrying out the Church's mission. Pope Francis, in keeping with the teachings of the Second Vatican Council, is trying to root out some of such stubborn, deeply entrenched attitudes and direct Christ's Church onto its true path.

In the past, evangelization was misperceived to be the work of a select few. Some Catholics thought (and many still do) that only Church professionals—bishops, priests, and religious—were responsible for evangelization, while those in the pews were to concern themselves with more mundane affairs. Clergy and religious were entrusted with the Church's missionary mandate of preaching, teaching, and sanctifying, while the rest of the faithful were to keep the commandments and be faithful to their responsibilities and vocational commitments. The laity were not considered active participants in the work of the gospel, but passive onlookers to be seen and not heard, and to do what they were told.

Old habits die hard. Recently, many parents thought that the primary responsibility for educating children in the faith rested with the parish priests and the religious sisters in the parish school. The parents got their children to church on Sunday, sending them to Catholic school or religious education class, and making sure they received the sacraments. Everything else was left to those "in charge"—and "in charge" they were! Not all that long ago the pastor's decisions for the parish or the school principal's disciplinary actions were never questioned, even when they were flawed or ineffective! There are many reasons for this misconception of evangelization's nature and scope, mainly because of a two-tiered (almost dichotomized) understanding of discipleship and the Christian call to holiness. The beatitudes were the way of life for clergy and religious, but everyone else was to obey the commandments. The former were the missionaries, evangelists, and catechists; the latter, those missionized, evangelized, and catechized. The distinction was clear: some were considered "super Christians," so-to-speak, and others ordinary, "run of the mill" Christians. Families were not considered "domestic churches,"[16] but receptacles to be filled with the Church's doctrinal and moral teachings by authoritative figures.

The Second Vatican Council clarified this misunderstanding by proclaiming "the universal call to holiness," depicting the entire Church as "a pilgrim people" on a journey to God.[17] This call and journey are at the heart of what it means to be a follower of Jesus. In this respect, all Christians—priests, religious, and laity—are called to the work of evangelization. All are called to the same primary mission, to spread the gospel, and do so in and through the community of faithful. Pope Francis puts it this way: "Evangelization is the task of the Church. The Church…is a people advancing on its pilgrim way toward God. She is certainly a mystery rooted in the Trinity, yet she exists concretely in history as a people of pilgrims and evangelizers, transcending any institutional expression, however necessary" (EG 111). God's people must seek the Spirit's guidance in all things and keep their eyes fixed on their final destination. If they do not, like the ancient Hebrews in Sinai (Nm 32:13), they will lose themselves in the desert wilderness they encounter along the way. They will lose their bearings and wander aimlessly through life without sense or purpose.

The Church's purpose, its reason for being, its "mission statement," if you will, is to "make disciples of all nations" (Mt 28:19).[18] For Francis, every believer shares in this mission, since the entire people of God proclaim the message (EG 111). Although the Church, as the body of Christ, has many members, each with a particular function within the body, all are still one and work together for a single purpose. St. Paul writes, "God has so arranged the body… that there may be no dissension within the body, but the members may have the same care for one another. If one member suffers, all suffer together with it; if one member is honored, all rejoice together with it" (1 Cor 12:24–26). Similarly, in the Church the members have different roles, but all are involved in the work of evangelization and building the kingdom of God. Pope Francis clarifies this:

> In virtue of their baptism, all the members of the People of God have become missionary disciples (cf. Mt 28:19). All the baptized, whatever their position in the Church or their level of instruction in the faith, are agents of evangelization, and it would not envisage a plan of evangelization to be carried out by professionals while the rest of the faithful would be passive recipients. The new evangelization calls for personal involvement by

each of the baptized. Every Christian is challenged, here and now, to be engaged in evangelization; anyone who has truly experienced God's saving love needs little time or lengthy training to proclaim that love. Every Christian is a missionary if he or she has encountered the love of God in Christ Jesus: we no longer say we are "disciples" and "missionaries," but rather that we are always "missionary disciples."

(EG 120)

Scripture itself testifies to this truth: "If the whole body were an eye, where would the hearing be? If the whole body were hearing, where would the sense of smell be?" (1 Cor 12:17). Elsewhere it states: "Like good stewards of the manifold grace of God, serve one another with whatever gift each of you has received. Whoever speaks must do so as one speaking the very words of God; whoever serves must do so with the strength that God supplies" (1 Pt 4:10–11). Evangelization is work that Christ and his Church do together. Pope Francis reminds us of this: "It is an absurd dichotomy to love Christ without the Church; to listen to Christ but not the Church; to be with Christ at the margins of the Church. One cannot do this. It is an absurd dichotomy."[19] As missionary disciples, we are each called to roles in the Church to serve God's purpose. We must mature in the work of evangelization so we can transmit the gospel in new ways and inculturate it in today's world. The Holy Spirit working through the Church is the principal agent of this evangelization, and culture is its primary medium. As the new evangelization unfolds, we are called to be in tune with the Spirit and so we can respond to God's promptings and understand how we can bring the gospel to people of every background and culture.

Evangelization proceeds through informal preaching that begins with personal dialogue, moves on to breaking open the Word of God, and then ends with prayer (EG 127–28). It involves witnessing to people from all walks of life and on every societal level. Expressions of popular spirituality and piety such as the worldwide Marian shrines (e.g., Lourdes, Fatima, Aparecida, Guadalupe), the rosary, Forty Hours devotion, and the Divine Mercy chaplet are effective instruments of evangelization, and are seen as "a spirituality incarnated in the culture of the lowly" (EG 123–26). The pope also calls for other efforts to establish a program of creative apologetics to bring the light of faith to the frontiers of human knowledge through dialogue with scientific and other intellectual circles on university campuses, both Catholic and secular (EG 132–34). Because the different charisms within the Church and theology itself are instruments of evangelization, they cannot be bound to a desk or left resting in an armchair (EG 133). Above all, "'there can be no true evangelization without the explicit proclamation of Jesus as Lord' and without 'the primacy of the proclamation of Jesus Christ in all evangelizing work'" (EG 110).

Preaching the Word

Preachers know that "A good homily can change a person's life for the better and a bad one, for the worse." This statement recalls something St. Alphonsus de Liguori (1696–1787) said:

> It is not enough to preach…it is necessary to preach in a proper manner. First, in order to preach well learning and study are necessary. He who preaches at random will do great harm to religion. Second, an exemplary life is necessary. The sermons of a man whose conduct excites contempt shall be despised.[20]

Preaching the Good News of Jesus Christ's merciful love, through words or witness, is a primary, irreplaceable means of evangelization. Because of its central role in communicating and spreading the faith, Pope Francis devotes considerable space to its important ministerial action and responsibility within the Church. He acknowledges that homilies can make both the faithful and their ordained ministers suffer: "the laity from having to listen to them and the clergy from having to preach them!" (EG 135). Preaching the gospel, one of the Church's most important responsibilities, should not be boring and lifeless, but a dynamic and penetrating encounter with God's Word. St. Paul states, "If I proclaim the gospel, this gives me no ground for boasting, for an obligation is laid on me, and woe to me if I do not proclaim the gospel!" (1 Cor 9:16).

In its broad sense, preaching takes many forms. Alan of Lille (1116/17–1202) once remarked that it takes place through the spoken word (homilies and sermons), the written word (books and treatises), and deeds (the living witness of Christian love).[21] The pope's namesake, Francis of Assisi (1181–1226), admonished his friars, "Preach the Gospel at all times, and when necessary, use words."[22] These examples suggest that in its general sense preaching is not confined to any one medium. Spreading the gospel through art or even social media can be preaching. Despite the multitude of a ways to proclaim the message, Pope Francis emphasizes that in its deepest sense preaching concerns the proclamation of the gospel through the spoken word. After all, according to St. Paul, "Faith comes from what is heard, and what is heard comes through the word of Christ" (Rom 10:17). Nothing can replace the explicit proclamation of God's Word.

In *The Joy of the Gospel*, Pope Francis devotes considerable space to the homily. This "touchstone for judging a pastor's closeness and ability to communicate to his people" (EG 135) is "a dialogue between God and his people, a dialogue in which the great deeds of salvation are proclaimed and the demands of the covenant are continually restated" (EG 137). The homily, the pope states, also "has special importance due to its Eucharistic context: it surpasses all forms of catechesis as the supreme moment in the dialogue between God and his people which lead up to sacramental communion" (EG 137). It is not meant to be entertainment. This is "a distinctive genre", since it is preaching situated within the framework of a liturgical celebration. It should be brief and avoid appearing to be a speech or lecture (EG 138). Since preachers speak on behalf of the Church, they must address the faithful "in the same way that a mother speaks to her child, knowing that the child trusts that what she is teaching is for his or her benefit, for children know that they are loved" (EG 139).

Preachers must try to set their listeners' hearts on fire: "A preaching which would be purely moralistic or doctrinaire, or one which turns into a lecture on biblical exegesis, detracts from this heart-to-heart communication which takes place in the homily" (EG 142). They must look beyond weaknesses and failings to see listeners as Jesus sees them (EG 141). Preaching must not communicate merely ideas or detached values, but synthesize what lies within the heart: "To speak from the heart means that our hearts must not just be on fire, but also enlightened by the fullness of revelation and by the path travelled by God's word in the heart of the Church and our faithful people throughout history" (EG 144).

The pope also emphasizes the importance of preparation, offering a method for doing so. Preachers should call upon the Holy Spirit in prayer, approach the text with a deep reverence for the truth, take care to study the meaning of the text with the greatest care, focus on the text's central message, relate that message to the entire teaching of the Church, and allow it to penetrate their own thoughts and feelings so it resonates in their hearts (EG 146–50). By personalizing the message, preachers allow God's word to penetrate their entire being and keep them from proclaiming God's message in a shallow, inauthentic way. St. Augustine suggests, "For now, treat the Scripture of God as the face of God. Melt in it presence."[23] "What is essential," the pope insists, "is that the preacher be certain that God loves him, that

Jesus Christ has saved him and that his love always has the last word" (EG 151). Preachers can achieve this through *lectio divina*. This practice of spiritual reading begins with studying the text in its literal meaning and then discerning how the words speak to one's own life. (EG 152). A preacher who does not allow God's word to penetrate his heart "will indeed be a false prophet, a fraud, a shallow impostor" (EG 151).

Sometimes, Sunday homilies can go over the parishioners' heads, as if they were being preached to in a foreign language. Good preachers must speak the language of their people. Besides allowing God's word to touch and penetrate his own heart, an effective homilist "also needs to keep his ear to the people and to discover what it is that the faithful need to hear" (EG 154). Preachers must contemplate not only the word, but also the people they serve (EG 154). This twofold contemplative activity enables them to connect the biblical text with the human situation and speak in a way that brings listeners farther along the way of salvation. Preaching in this way demands spiritual sensitivity and discernment. Preachers must know their congregations' concerns and speak in a way that meets them where they are and leads them into a deeper, more authentic relationship with the Lord. They must avoid technical language and use homiletic resources in a way that respects the content of evangelization and its method. A good homily, the pope says, should have three things: "an idea, a sentiment, an image" (EG 157). It should use simple, positive language, not pointing out people's mistakes but suggesting what they can do better (EG

159). Preachers must be careful not to impose their own language and way of thinking on their audience. They must strive to speak so people understand and that resonates in their hearts.

Understanding the Kerygma

Some have said that "Christianity is not taught, but caught." This statement suggests that communicating the faith involves not only conveying doctrinal and moral teachings, but also bringing the message of Christ to others through a living witness—to give witness is to teach. A story about St. Clement Hofbauer (1751–1820) illustrates this point. After entering a tavern in Warsaw to beg money to support his refuge for homeless boys, an angry patron spat in his face. Hofbauer wiped off the spittle and said, "That was for me. Now what do you have for my boys?" Clement's humility so moved the men that they collected a large sum of silver to support the boys under his care.[24]

According to Pope Francis, a homily should help people understand their relationship with Christ by combining words with a witness of living faith. *Kerygma* is the proclamation of this living relationship. It seeks to engender doctrinal formation by encouraging people to grow in virtue by embracing the Lord's commandment to love one another as he has loved us (Jn 15:12). On our own we cannot love as Christ loved; it is a gift from God. The homily should help those who listen recognize their limitations and accept the gift of God's love that empowers them to love as he does. "All Christian formation," according to the pope, "consists of entering more deeply into the kerygma" (EG 165). The central message of the kerygma must be emphasized :

> [I]t has to express God's saving love which precedes any moral and religious obligation on our part; it should not impose the truth but appeal to freedom; it should be marked by joy, encouragement, liveliness and a harmonious balance which will not reduce preaching to a few doctrines which are at times more philosophical than evangelical.
>
> (EG 165)

True catechesis, he continues, lies in proclaiming the word. In its heart it is *kerygmatic*, focusing on God's mercy and love made manifest in the person of Jesus Christ. It is *mystagogic* because it involves "a progressive experience of formation involving the entire community and a renewed appreciation of the liturgical signs of Christian initiation" (EG 166). It attends to the "way of beauty" (*via pulchritudinis*) by encouraging the arts and by discovering new forms of beauty in cultural settings that will draw people to the true meaning of the gospel. Its moral component should be presented not as an end but as a response to the call of discipleship. Preaching should stress the positive message of the gospel: "Rather than experts in dire predictions, dour judges bent on rooting out every threat and deviation, we should appear as joyful messengers of challenging proposals, guardians of the goodness and beauty which shine forth in a life of fidelity to the Gospel" (EG 168).

As understanding of the kerygma deepens, the Church "will have to initiate everyone—priests, religious, and laity—into the 'art of accompaniment' which teaches us to remove our sandals before the sacred ground of the other" (EG 169). Spiritual accompaniment keeps believers from becoming spiritual drifters who wander away from God. It encourages them in their pilgrimage to the Father and teaches them to become proficient in the "art of listening" (EG 171). Centered and nourished by God's word, it helps them appropriate the divine mystery and continue the mission of evangelization. It helps them trust more deeply in God's word and encourages them to ponder God's self-revelation to them.

Conclusion

Pope Francis wants his readers to look forward by looking back. He calls them back to the Church's primary mission: the work of evangelization, proclaiming the Christian faith by giving witness to it. This work flows from the heart of the Church and forms a part of her sacred identity as the New Eve, the mother of redeemed humanity. Created in the image and likeness of God, this humanity mirrors God's own life, a community of love that pours itself out the threefold work of creation, redemption, and sanctification. This work manifests itself in the historical narrative of God's people and continues in the encounter between God's people and the world. The Church, a community of missionary disciples, is called to bear God's love to others. Through this community God continues "to make all things new" (Rev 21:5) by conforming humanity to the image and likeness of the Son through the power of the Spirit.

Pope Francis places the new evangelization at the forefront of the Church's awareness, asking the faithful to discover how they can contribute to it. Every believer shares in the life and mission of the Church and plays an important role in bringing Christ to others at this moment in history. The work of evangelization, the pope says, involves leading others to a personal, face-to-face encounter with Christ. That cannot happen unless those who lead have not first experienced the joy of such an intimate relationship. He points out, therefore, that Christians themselves must be evangelized anew, setting their own hearts on fire with the love of God and being filled with a longing to preach the gospel in all they think, say, and do. God is passionately in love with humankind, Pope Francis says, and asks every person to reciprocate that divine love by expressing it to others.

The new evangelization brings Christ to those who may never have heard his message or who have not allowed it to touch their hearts and penetrate their very being. It proclaims Jesus Christ within and beyond the community of faith, constantly seeking new ways of proclaiming the Good News of God's merciful love. To bring the gospel message to the world through inculturation, the faithful must travel great distances, not only physically but also mentally, spiritually, and culturally. To do this, they must take all that is good in the world, imbue it with the Spirit of Christ, and make it their own. They must tear down barriers of hatred and division and build bridges between people, and between them and God. The new evangelization is a loving and joyful proclamation that extends to anyone searching for the meaning of life and who wishes to live accordingly.

Reflection Questions

* What does the new evangelization mean to you? How does it differ from the old evangelization?

* What role are you supposed to play in it? How do you figure out what that role is? What are the methods of the new evangelization? What place does proclamation of Jesus Christ have in it? How are you a missionary disciple?

* Why must the gospel message be expressed in new ways? Why is it important that the gospel be inculturated? What practical methods of evangelization can you employ in your home, your community, your workplace?

4

Life in Communion

The mystery of the Trinity reminds us we have been created in the image of that divine communion, and so we cannot achieve fulfillment or salvation purely by our own efforts. From the heart of the Gospel we see the profound connection between evangelization and human advancement, which must find expression and develop in every work of evangelization. Accepting the first proclamation, which invites us to receive God's love and to love him in return with the love which is his gift, brings forth in our lives and actions a primary and fundamental response: to desire, seek and protect the good of others.

Evangelii Gaudium, 178

"He called the twelve and began to send them out two by two and gave them authority over unclean spirits" (Mk 6:7). This passage makes the nature of the new evangelization clear: it is a work of Christ and his body, the Church, and therefore preeminently communal. Jesus sent his disciples out not alone, but in groups of two or three. He did so because evangelization, which flows from the heart of God is, before all else, the work of the intimate community of divine love. Jesus' mission stems from his intimate relationship with the Father and the Holy Spirit, given to the community of disciples at Pentecost, empowering the Church to spread the Good News of God's love for humanity to every corner of the earth (Acts 1:8; 2:1–13). Disciples proclaim to others that God is love in and through their mutual love—love generously given and humbly received.

Since it flows from the heart of the Trinity, the new evangelization continues God's own creative, redemptive, and sanctifying work. It builds the kingdom by forming community and caring for society. Christians evangelize the world by embracing and transforming it through the power of God's love. Love for God and neighbor are intimately bound: "[I]f we love one another, God lives in us, and his love is perfected in us" (1 Jn 4:12). It is the communitarian nature of the new evangelization that Pope Francis wishes to emphasize.

Reaching Society

To discover the original human language, a curious (yet insensitive) scholar kidnapped an infant and raised it to the age of reason in complete isolation. As he grew, the child's physical needs were provided for—food, clothing, shelter—but he could not see, touch, or communicate with any other human being.

This crude, heartless "experiment" produced a wild child of six or seven who could not relate to others and could not use language at all! The lack of human contact stunted the child's mental growth and development. This cold-hearted experiment confirms that self-identity develops through relationship with others.

Although it may be apocryphal, the story's point is clear: Human beings are social by nature and discover their identity through relationships. As the Vatican II document *Lumen Gentium* states, "God... does not make men holy and save them merely as individuals, without bond or link between one another. Rather has it pleased him to bring men together as one people, a people which acknowledges Him and serves him in holiness."[25] Therefore, spreading the gospel cannot focus solely on one's individual relationship with Christ. The gospel has personal and social dimensions. Because God is love (1 Jn 4:8) and because this message of love lies at the heart of the Good News, evangelization must seek to make that love visible and real in the lives of the people we serve. Pope Francis emphasizes this social dimension, cautioning us of the "constant risk of distorting the authentic and integral meaning of the mission of evangelization" (EG 176).

"The kerygma," the pope states, "has a clear social content" (EG177). This content is not a lesser, secondary element of the gospel message; it is central: "Our redemption has a social dimension because 'God, in Christ, redeems not only the individual person, but also the social relations existing between men'" (EG

177). As Aristotle attests, "Man is by nature a social animal."[26] Human nature is social. For us to experience the fullness of God's love, our social ties must be transformed. These ties include not only our close, interpersonal relationships among family and friends, but also the associations and social structures through which we organize ourselves. The gospel penetrates every dimension of human existence: "To believe that the Holy Spirit is at work in everyone means realizing that he seeks to penetrate every human situation and all social bonds" (EG 177).

The challenge of the new evangelization, for Pope Francis, is to recognize that the missionary nature of the Church requires us to contact others. We would be mistaken to consider this challenge "simply... an accumulation of small personal gestures to individuals in need, a kind of 'charity à la carte,' or a series of acts aimed solely at easing our conscience" (EG 180). Missionary discipleship means more than digging into our pockets or writing a check. It is even more than St. Martin of Tours cutting his cloak in two to cover a naked man in the dead of winter, or St. Francis of Assisi kissing and embracing a leper, or even Pope Francis hugging a visibly disfigured man during a weekly audience. As commendable as these acts are, the gospel of Christ asks much more: "Its mandate of charity encompasses all dimensions of existence, all individuals, all areas of community life, and all peoples. Nothing human can be alien to it" (EG 181). Evangelization must reach beyond the private sphere into "the complexities of current situations"(EG 183). It stems from God's desire that we be happy both in this life and in the next and from authentic faith that "always involves a deep desire to change the world, to transmit values, to leave this earth somehow better than we found it" (EG 180).

The pope admits that neither he nor the Church has "a monopoly on the interpretation of social realities or the proposal of solutions to contemporary problems" (EG 184). Nor does he spell out the Church's social teaching, since that information is readily available (EG 184).[27] He also recognizes that it is "up to the Christian communities to analyze with objectivity the situation which is proper to their own country" (EG 184). He wishes, however, to contribute some constructive insights concerning our present situation. To do so, he focuses on two central issues: "the inclusion of the poor in society" and "peace and social dialogue" (EG 185).

Loving the Poor

A stranger entered a village with nothing but a large black kettle and a spoon. At the center of the village square he placed his kettle on a stand, put in it a stone, filled it with water, then built a fire beneath it. When passers-by asked him what he was doing, he smiled and said, "I'm making soup!" "You can't make soup without vegetables. You need some peas and carrots," said one person. "What about some potatoes?" asked another. "What about some chicken?" offered yet another. Before long, all the villagers had provided ingredients. And all the while, the stranger did nothing but stir! In time, he had cooked up a hearty soup he shared with everyone, especially the poor and needy.

We need to encourage others to improve society according to genuine human values that conform to the mind of Christ. At the heart of the gospel is a humble God who "emptied himself, taking the form of a slave, being born in human likeness" (Phil 2:7–8). In this act of self-emptying, Jesus was poor to enrich humanity with the gift of divine life. We must seek to do the same. Pope Francis puts it this way: "Our faith in Christ, who became poor and was always close to them, is the basis of our concern for the integral development of society's most neglected members" (EG 186). As the community of disciples that bears his name, embraces his life, and seeks to follow his teachings, the Church follows Jesus' example: "Each individual Christian and every community is called to be an instrument of God for the liberation and promotion of the poor, and for enabling them to be fully a part of society" (EG 187). A lack of solidarity with the poor diminishes our relationship with God: "How does God's love abide in anyone who has the world's goods, and sees a brother or sister in need and yet refuses help?" (1 Jn 3:17).

Contacting the poor, for Pope Francis, "means working to eliminate the structural causes of poverty and to promote the integral development of the poor, as well as small daily acts of solidarity in meeting the real needs which we encounter" (EG 188). It extends beyond isolated acts of generosity to true solidarity with the poor, fostering convictions and habits that restore their dignity and serve the common good.

Putting on "the mind of Christ"(1 Cor 2:16) means embracing Jesus' preferential option for the poor and recognizing that by evangelizing them we are also evangelized (EG 198). It asks us to recognize that the planet on which we live belongs to all humanity and that all persons, wherever they live or whatever their resources, have a right to its benefits. The pope says that all are called "to hear the cry of the poor," to help them along the road to self-fulfillment (EG 190–91), even if it demands that "the more fortunate should renounce some of their rights so as to place their goods more generously at the service of others" (EG 190). We are asked to reduce our wastefulness so more resources might be used on behalf of the poor. It means working to ensure both "'a dignified sustenance' for all people" and "their 'general welfare and prosperity,'" especially by ensuring access to adequate education, health care, employment, and a just wage (EG 192), providing for their spiritual needs, and extending the Lord's invitation of mercy and forgiveness (EG 193, 200).

Pope Francis challenges us not to succumb to a "new self-centered paganism," begging us to remember the poor, which is an important measure of our faithfulness to the gospel (EG 195). God's heart has a special place for the poor, who are present throughout salvation history (EG 197). He wants the Church to exercise an option for the poor by being poor herself and working on their behalf (EG 198). The poor have much to teach us. By contemplating their faces we see the face of Christ (EG 199). The members of the Church are not to get lost in aimless and uncontrolled activism, but moved by the Holy Spirit to attend to the needs of the poor and to alleviate their suffering. Such action involves an authentic option for the poor that differs from ideology or exploiting them for personal gain. It embraces the poor, seeks to lift them out of their poverty, and to make them feel at home in the Christian community (EG 199). "Without the preferential option for the poor, 'the proclamation of the Gospel…risks being misunderstood or submerged in an ocean of words which daily engulfs us in today's society of mass communications'" (EG 199).

No one is exempt from concern for the poor: "'Spiritual conversion, the intensity of the love of God and neighbor, zeal for justice and peace, the Gospel meaning of the poor and of poverty, are required of everyone'" (EG 201). By recognizing Christ in our neighbor, especially in the poor and marginalized, we recognize Christ himself, who said: "'Truly I tell you, just as you did it to one of the least of these who are members of my family, you did it to me'" (Mt 25:40). This commitment to the poor requires us to have a concrete effect in their lives. The pope calls for renewed efforts to create a healthy world economy that preserves the common good and honors the dignity of every human person (EG 203). He calls not for temporary help for the poor, but for systematic change: "As long as the problems of the poor are not radically resolved by rejecting the absolute autonomy of markets and financial speculation and by attacking the structural causes of inequality, no solution will be found for the world's problems or, for that matter, to any problems" (EG 202). "Inequality," he says, "is the root of social ills" (EG 202). Rather than merely trusting in invisible market forces, he believes that growth in justice "requires decisions, programs, mechanisms and processes specifically geared to a better distribution of income, the creation of sources of employment and an integral promotion of the poor which goes beyond a simple welfare mentality" (EG 204). Every government shares in the responsibility for creating an environment that "ensures the economic well-being of all countries, not just of a few" (EG 206). Just what these decisions, programs, mechanisms, and processes might be he leaves for experts to discern and implement. He insists, however, that economic systems stem from a genuine concern to elevate the situation of the poor rather than using (and even exploiting) them to increase the wealth of a relative few.

Pope Francis understands that his words may offend some, even though he pronounces them with love and affection. His primary purpose is to remind us that Jesus closely identifies with the poor and those who follow Christ "are called to care for the vulnerable of the earth" (EG 209). After all, Jesus himself said, "Blessed are you who are poor, for yours is the kingdom of God" (Lk 6:20). These poor include "the homeless, the addicted, refugees, indigenous peoples, the elderly who are increasingly isolated and abandoned, and many others" (EG 210). They also include migrants, victims of human trafficking (children, prostitutes, the undocumented), women subjected to mistreatment and violence, and the unborn (EG

210–14). The pope asks us to defend the weak and defenseless and bids us to increase our efforts to preserve our environment so future generations may be able to benefit from and enjoy the fruits of the earth (EG 215). "[A]ll of us, as Christians are called to watch over and protect the fragile world in which we live, and all its peoples" (EG 216).

Dialogue for Peace

Life in communion also includes "peace and social dialogue." One of the sad paradoxes of our age of technology and instant communication is that more people have forgotten how to listen. This tendency applies not only to individuals, but also to corporate bodies like religions and nations. Rather than talking past one another without acknowledging that others are speaking, we need to set aside our personal concerns and listen to those with whom we disagree. Without communication we will not find peace, in this world or in the next. Faith comes through hearing: "Let anyone with ears to hear listen!" (Mk 4:9).

In the Sermon on the Mount Jesus says, "Blessed are the peacemakers" (Mt 5:9). Pope Francis points out that peace, a fruit of the gospel, "cannot be understood as pacification or the mere absence of violence resulting from the domination of one part of society over others" (EG 218). "True peace," he says, cannot "act as a pretext for justifying a social structure which silences or appeases the poor, so that the more affluent can placidly support their lifestyle while others have to make do as they can" (EG 218).

Nor is peace "simply the mere absence of warfare, based on a precarious balance of power"; instead, it must be "fashioned by efforts directed day after day toward the establishment of the ordered universe willed by God, with a more perfect justice among men" (EG 219). Such efforts must be well ordered and focused on outcomes.

Authentic dialogue takes place in charity, against a backdrop of silence in service to the truth. This quiet ground of conversation must be tended carefully, allowing the partners in dialogue to formulate their ideas and share them in an honest and respectful manner. Chiara Lubich, the founder of the Focolare Movement, puts it this way:

> Dialogue means that people meet together and even though they have different ideas, they speak with serenity and sincere love toward the other person to find some kind of agreement that can clarify misunderstandings, calm disputes, resolve conflicts, and even eliminate hatred. This dialogue, especially among the faithful of different religions, today is more indispensable than ever if we want to avoid the great evils threatening our societies.[28]

To this same end the pope offers four basic principles for promoting a dialogue for peace: (1) "Time is greater than space." (2) "Unity prevails over conflict." (3) "Realities are more important than ideas." And (4) "The whole is greater than the part" (EG 222–37). "Peace," St. Augustine says, "is the tranquility of order," which begins in this life and reaches its fulfillment in the world to come.[29] These four principles, the pope asserts, "can guide the development of life in society and the building of a people where differences are harmonized within a shared pursuit" (EG 221). When implemented they can bring about authentic and true "tranquility of order," for which everyone yearns.

Each of these principles contributes something unique to building peace. The first asks us "to work slowly but surely, without being obsessed with immediate results" so we can be more "concerned about initiating processes rather than possessing spaces" (EG 223). The second invites us "to build communion amid disagreement," to recognize that "unity is greater than conflict," and to strive for "the building of friendship in society" (EG 228). The third reminds us that ideas must not mask or be disconnected from reality, but be rooted in it to serve and improve it (EG 231–32). The fourth asserts that to avoid banality and narrowness of mind, we need to consider the entire picture (EG 234). Doing so helps us respect the whole and the parts, gives us a healthy respect for local and global events, and allows us to see the connections between them.

According to the pope, by using these four principles we can work patiently toward the new evangelization. It can be established by inculturating the gospel in concrete, practical ways that unify the nations of the earth through gospel love. They establish a context for constructive dialogue that leads to peace. They embody what Pope St. John XXIII yearned for in *Pacem in Terris* and sought to establish through the Second Vatican Council:

> Let us pray with all fervor for this peace which our divine Redeemer came to bring us. May He banish from the souls of men whatever might endanger peace. May He transform all men into witnesses of truth, justice and brotherly love. May He illumine with His light the minds of rulers, so that, besides caring for the proper material welfare of their peoples, they may also guarantee them the fairest gift of peace.[30]

Pope Francis outlines a program of dialogue by which the new evangelization can promote human development for the sake of peace and the common good. This program proposes active participation, patient listening, and mutual exchange of ideas on a variety of levels: "dialogue with states, dialogue with society—including dialogue with cultures and the sciences—and dialogue with other believers who are not part of the Catholic Church" (EG 238). As it seeks to cooperate with these various groups to promote the universal good of society, the Church offers to the discussion the light of faith and a wealth of experience.

Since Jesus Christ is peace itself (Eph 2:14), "the new evangelization calls on every baptized person to be a peacemaker and a credible witness to a reconciled life" (EG 239). The Church, according to the pope, must work with local, national, and international governments "to safeguard and promote the common good of society" (EG 239). Although the Church may not have concrete solutions for particular issues, the Christian community defends the dignity of the human person and promotes the common good in the various sectors of society (EG 241). Concerning a topic related to the common good, the relationship between faith and science, the pope calls for the new evangelization to maintain an open dialogue: "Faith is not fearful of reason; on the contrary, it seeks and trusts reason, since 'the light of reason and the light of faith both come from God' and cannot contradict each other" (EG 242).

The new evangelization also includes the Church's dialogue with other Christian communities, Jews, Muslims, Hindus, Buddhists, people of other faiths, those not associated with any religious faith tradition, atheists, and all seekers of truth (EG 250–54). In a "dialogue of charity" with such groups, religious and non-religious alike, the Church must speak the truth with tenderness and love. In these conversations, the faithful must condemn violence as way of resolving conflict, avoid any facile syncretism, expose all narrow rationalism, confront the dictatorship of relativism, warn against purely individual religious experiences, and promote authentic religious freedom (EG 255–58). In doing so, we must listen and respond, speaking with respect for the dignity of the other's point of view and a sincere desire for the good of society.

Conclusion

According to Pope Francis, because the gospel embraces every reality it must extend beyond the personal to every dimension of human society. The implications of Jesus' message, "Go into all the world and proclaim the good news to the whole creation"

(Mk 16:15) extend beyond mere geography. The gospel must be proclaimed not only to the four corners of the earth, but also to every dimension of human existence itself, including the societal. The challenge of the new evangelization is to bring the message of Christ to society by promoting peace and social justice among all of humanity through dialogue with various social entities (e.g., the state, scientific institutions, other religious traditions).

Pope Francis outlines two key areas where the new evangelization must engage human society: "including the poor in society" and "working for peace and social dialogue." As followers of Jesus, we are called to imitate him by making a preferential option for the poor and promoting their full development. We do this not by sporadic acts of charity to ease our consciences, but by working to change the structures of social injustice that prevent the poor from rising above their poverty and taking their rightful place in society. For this to happen, the world's economic structures must be changed to promote equality rather than subjugation of the many to a select few. Even though he does not pretend to propose concrete solutions to complex societal and economic issues, the pope realizes that many will resist his challenge. Nor is he willing to embrace simplistic solutions such as a welfare state that perpetuates rather than alleviates the troubled lot of the poor. Although he understands there will always be poor among us (Mk 14:7), he issues this challenge out of love and affection for all humanity, reminding us that all true followers of Christ love the poor and have their best interests at heart.

These interests are best advanced through dialogue with those who hold positions of power and those who take perspectives that differ from those of Christ and his Church. Through conversation with various state, scientific, and religious groups, the pope believes the new evangelization can build bonds of friendship that will promote social justice and the universal good. Besides dialogue, he offers four principles that can help the Church promote unity patiently, realistically, and without conflict. Although the kingdom of God lies beyond this life, the pope insists that it is being built in the here-and-now. He preaches peace, justice, and unity; he asks all believers, and all people of good will, to take it to heart.

Reflection Questions

- Why must the gospel be oriented toward society and not merely toward the individual? What does this orientation say about God's love?

- What do you consider to be the gospel?

- What is your relationship with the poor? How do you regard them? Why is the preferential option for the poor so important for the new evangelization? What concrete steps can you take in your daily life to contact the poor and marginalized?

- Why is no one exempt from promoting peace and social justice in society? What concrete steps can you take to advance peace and justice in your community?

Conclusion

A Work of the Spirit

Spirit-filled evangelizers means evangelizers fearlessly open to the working of the Holy Spirit. At Pentecost, the Spirit made the apostles go forth from themselves and turned them into heralds of God's wondrous deeds, capable of speaking to each person in his or her own language. The Holy Spirit also grants the courage to proclaim the newness of the Gospel with boldness (*parrhesía*) in every time and place, even when it meets with opposition. Let us call upon him today, firmly rooted in prayer, for without prayer all our activity risks being fruitless and our message empty. Jesus wants evangelizers who proclaim the good news not only with words, but above all by a life transfigured by God's presence.

Evangelii Gaudium, 259

*T*he Holy Spirit is the author of the new evangelization and Mary is its mother. Together, they inspire the Church and all the faithful to be courageous,

Spirit-filled missionary disciples. The Spirit is the bond of love between the Father and the Son; Mary, the faithful disciple who followed the Lord from the beginning to the end of his earthly life—and into eternity. We followers of Christ are all called to do our part in the work of the new evangelization, rooted in the Spirit, indebted to Mary Our Mother, and focused on the mission Jesus has laid before us.

Jesus clarified the Church's mission: "Go, therefore, and make disciples of all nations" (Mt 28:19). This mandate touches the heart of the Church; Jesus' own mission shapes the Church's identity. From the beginning Christians have spread the Good News of Jesus' triumph over death. As we enter the third millennium, we follow them in embracing the gospel with every fiber of our being and preaching it to the ends of the earth.

Filled with the Spirit

Pope Francis envisions a new era of evangelization, a time when all Church members will be open to the working of the Holy Spirit, and will boldly proclaim the Good News of Jesus Christ to the world. For this to happen, we must be firmly rooted in prayer, "for without [it] all our activity risks being fruitless and our message empty" (EG 259). He ends his commentary on the new evangelization reflecting on its underlying spirit (EG 260), imploring the Holy Spirit "to come and renew the Church, to stir and impel her to go forth boldly to evangelize all peoples" (EG 261).

Francis insists that all Christians are called to be "Spirit-filled evangelizers," our missionary outreach fueled by our personal encounter with Jesus (EG 262). We must deepen our relationship with the Lord and contact others in a spirit of generosity and service. A renewed missionary impulse can take shape within the Church if we quiet ourselves to hear the promptings of the Spirit in our lives and respond by working in concrete and practical ways. Francis sees this impulse being carried out in the Church and welcomes its continued growth: "The Church urgently needs the deep breath of prayer, and to my great joy groups devoted to prayer and intercession, the prayerful reading of God's word and the perpetual adoration of the Eucharist are growing at every level of ecclesial life" (EG 195). He asks us to reject false spirituality, especially forms overly privatized and which focus too much on the individual. Because every period of human history has presented challenges to missionary efforts, he urges we learn from the saints, emulating them in ways suitable for our own day (EG 263).

Like the saints, we evangelize because we love Jesus. This love enkindles our desire to share it with others: "If we do not feel an intense desire to share this love, we need to pray insistently that he will once more touch our hearts" (EG 264). We need to recover a contemplative spirit that ponders the gospel and allows it to touch our hearts. Remember that we were created for the gospel and that it responds to our deepest needs, offering us "friendship with Jesus and love for our brothers and sisters" (EG 265). Each person we meet already has "an expectation, even if an unconscious one, of knowing the truth about God, about man, and about how we are to be set free from sin and death" (EG 265). Our enthusiasm for evangelization must be rooted in this conviction and "sustained by our own constantly renewed experience of savoring Christ's friendship and message" (EG 266). As missionary disciples, we must never stop walking with Jesus in this way: "A person who is not convinced, enthusiastic, certain and in love, will convince nobody" (EG 266). As his disciples, we must live in union with Jesus as "we seek what he seeks and love what he loves" (EG 267). We must remain close to his heart, just as he remains close to his Father's heart.

Our love for Jesus manifests itself in our love and concern for his people. "Mission," the pope says, "is at once a passion for Jesus and a passion for his people" (EG 268). One passion serves the other: "Jesus is the model of this method of evangelization which brings us to the very heart of his people" (EG 269). Our closeness to him kindles in us a desire to be close to his people. Jesus' death on the cross was the culmination of a life lived totally for others, and we are called to follow. He wants us to engage with others, to enter into the reality of their lives in a kind and gentle manner. He calls us "to touch human misery, to touch the suffering flesh of others" (EG 270). Our own happiness lies in seeking the good of others and desiring happiness for them (EG 272). Every person is an object of God's infinite tenderness and worthy of love and respect (EG 274).

"Jesus truly lives," the pope says. If we believed this, we would set aside the destructive attitudes which tell us that nothing will ever change and focus instead on the reality of Jesus' triumph over sin and death (EG 275). We would find in the Risen and Glorified Lord everything we believed in, hoped for, and acted upon. We would believe "that he truly loves us, that he is alive, that he is mysteriously capable of intervening, that he does not abandon us and that he brings good out of evil by his power and his infinite creativity" (EG 278). Also, we would believe that he acts in and through us by the power of his Spirit, who frees us for mission, who "works as he wills, when he wills and where he wills" (EG 280). We would also appreciate more the power of intercessory prayer, which is not "a diversion from true contemplation" (EG 281), but "a 'leaven' in the heart of the Trinity" (EG 283) and a powerful instrument of evangelization (EG 281).

Turning to Mary

Pope Francis has a special devotion to Mary as "Our Lady, Undoer of Knots." For him, Mary "is the Mother who patiently and lovingly brings us to God, so that he can untangle the knots of our soul."[31] This devotion is especially appropriate for the missionary disciples of the new evangelization. To evangelize the world we ourselves must first be evangelized. Only if we first humbly ask the Lord to untie the tangled knots of our own souls will we be able to help untie the myriad entanglements in which the world finds itself. Once we are freed from our own restraints we can help others untie the knots within their souls.

As he concludes his reflection on the new evangelization, Pope Francis calls upon Mary and entrusts the Church to her care and protection. He tells us that Jesus gave the Church the gift of his mother when he entrusted her to the beloved disciple (Jn 19:26–27). He highlights the close relationship between Mary and the Church; just as she gave birth to the Son of God, so are we called to bear him both within our hearts and in the love we extend to others.

Mary shares our history and represents the fulfillment of our deepest dreams and hopes. She embodies "a Marian 'style' to the Church's work of evangelization" (EG 288). She was with the disciples as they waited for the Holy Spirit (Acts 1:14) and made possible the Church's first missionary efforts: "She is the Mother of the Church which evangelizes, and without her we could never truly understand the spirit of the new evangelization" (EG 284). Chiara Lubich explains what she and her companions came to understand about Mary's style of evangelization, how she so nourished herself on scripture that her every word and action transmitted Christ:

> She [Mary], set as a rare and unique creature within the Holy Trinity, was all Word of God, all dressed in the Word of God. And so strong was our impression of this understanding that it seemed to us that only angels could utter something of her.
>
> If, in fact, the Word is the splendor of the Father, Mary, so imbued with the Word of God,

appeared to us as having incomparable beauty.

And it is the Magnificat that tells us how Mary is all Word of God, as it is a continuous succession of words from scripture: the Virgin Mary was so nourished by the scriptures that in her speaking she was accustomed to use its very same expressions.

And it appeared so clear to us that what characterized Mary, though in her unique perfection, should characterize every Christian: to repeat Christ, the Truth, with the personality given to each by God.[32]

Mary reveals "the revolutionary nature of love and tenderness" (EG 288). She "is able to recognize the traces of God's Spirit in events great and small. She constantly contemplates the mystery of God in our world, in human history and in our daily lives. She is the woman of prayer and work in Nazareth, and she is also Our Lady of Help, who sets out from her town with haste (Lk 1:39) to be of service to others" (EG 288). She is the model of a Spirit-filled disciple. She, the first to experience the fullness of God's redemptive love, is the star of the new evangelization. We turn to her as we seek to open this new chapter in the Church's evangelizing efforts. We look to her as the "Mother of the living Gospel" (EG 288) and ask her to be with us and to help us as we contact others and draw them closer to her Son.

Notes

1 Pope Francis, *Evangelium Gaudium* ("Apostolic Exhortation on the Proclamation of the Gospel in Today's World," November 24, 2013), The Holy See, http://www.vatican.va/holy_father/francesco/apost_exhortations/documents/papa-francesco_esortazione-ap_20131124_evangelii-gaudium_en.html (accessed March 10, 2014). Referred throughout the text as EG.

2 Pope Francis, "Homily for Holy Thursday" (March 13, 2013), The Holy See, http://www.vatican.va/holy_father/francesco/homilies/2013/documents/papa-francesco_20130328_messa-crismale_en.html (accessed March 10, 2014).

3 Unless noted otherwise, Scripture quotations come from The *New Revised Standard Version* (National Council of the Churches of Christ, 1989).

4 Thomas Aquinas, *Summa theologiae*, II-II, q. 30, a. 4

5 Francis Thompson, "The Hound of Heaven," in *The Liturgy of the Hours*, vol. 4 (New York: Catholic Book Publishing Co., 1975), 2002–6.

6 See Frederick Jones, ed., *Alphonsus de Liguori: Selected Writings, The Classics of Western Spirituality* (New York/Mahwah, NJ: Paulist Press, 1999), 268.

7 See Thomas Reese, "Pope Francis and the Three Temptations of the Church," *National Catholic Reporter* (August 13, 2013), http://ncronline.org/news/spirituality/pope-francis-and-three-temptations-church (accessed March 10, 2014).

8 See Sherry A. Weddell, *Forming Intentional Disciples: The Path to Knowing and Following Jesus* (Huntington, IN: Our Sunday Visitor, 2012), 46.

9 See "I Dare Ya," in *Lessons in Motivation & Inspiration from MJD* (Thursday, May 29, 2008), http://coach-

mjd.blogspot.com//2008/06/i-dare-ya.html (accessed March 10, 2014).

10 C.S. Lewis, *The Abolition of Man* (New York: Macmillan, 1947), 88.

11 See Paul Wadell, *Friendship and the Moral Life* (Notre Dame, IN: University of Notre Dame Press, 1988), 130–41.

12 Alphonsus de Liguori, *The Way of Salvation and Perfection* in *The Complete Ascetical Works of St. Alphonsus de Liguori*, ed. Eugene Grimm, vol. 2 (Brooklyn, St. Louis, Toronto: Redemptorist Fathers, 1926), 395.

13 Jorge Mario Bergoglio and Abraham Skorka, *On Heaven and Earth: Pope Francis on Faith, Family, and the Church in the Twenty-First Century*, trans. Alejandro Bermudez and Howard Goodman (New York: Image, 2013), 55.

14 Ibid., 58.

15 Aristotle, *Metaphysics*, 2.

16 See the Second Vatican Council, *Lumen Gentium*, ("The Dogmatic Constitution on the Church," November 21, 1964), no. 11, The Holy See, http://www.vatican.va/archive/hist_councils/ii_vatican_council/ documents/vat-ii const 19641121_lumen-gentium_en.html (accessed March 10, 2014).

17 Ibid., nos. 39, 48,

18 See Michael White and Tom Corcoran, *Rebuilt: Awakening the Faithful, Reaching the Lost, and Making Church Matter* (Notre Dame, IN: Ave Maria Press, 2013), 38–39.

19 Pope Francis, "Daily Homily for January 30, 2014." Cited in *Aleteia*, http://www.aleteia.org/ en/religion/aggregated-content/a-christian-without-the-church-is-an-absurd-dichotomy-says-pope-5879481193463808?utm_campaign=NL_en&utm_

source=daily_newsletter&utm_medium=mail&utm_content=NL_en-31/01/2014 (accessed March 10 2014).

20 Alphonsus de Liguori, *Dignity and Duties of the Priest or Selva*, in *The Complete Works of St. Alphonsus de Liguori*, ed. Eugene Grimm, vol. 12 (Brooklyn/St. Louis/Toronto: Redemptorist Fathers, 1927), 266.

21 Alan of Lille, *The Art of Preaching*, trans. Gillian R. Evans, Cistercian Studies Series no. 23 (Kalamazoo, MI: Cistercian Publications, 1981), 20.

22 Attributed to Francis of Assisi, http://www.goodreads.com/quotes/7763-preach-the-gospel-at-all-times-and-when-necessary-use (accessed March 10, 2014).

23 Augustine of Hippo, Sermon 22.7 in *The Works of St. Augustine: Sermons*, trans. Edward Hill, vol. 1 (New York, 1990), 41–48. See also Robert Louis Wilken, *The Spirit of Early Christian Thought* (New Haven/London: Yale University Press, 2003), 50.

24 See "The Redemptorists: Saint Clement Hofbauer," http://www.cssr.com/english/saints blessed/ sthofbauer.shtml (accessed March 10, 2014).

25 Second Vatican Council, *Lumen Gentium*, no. 9

26 Aristotle, *Politics*, Bk. 1, sect. 1253a.

27 See, for example, The Pontifical Council of Justice and Peace, *The Compendium of the Social Doctrine of the Church* (June 29, 2004), The Holy See, http://www.vatican.va/roman_curia/pontifical_councils/justpeace/documents/rc_pc_justpeace_doc_20060526_compendio-dott-soc_en.html (accessed March 10, 2014).

28 Chiara Lubich, "360° Dialogue," in *Essential Writings: Spirituality, Dialogue, Culture*, ed. Michel Vandeleene (Hyde Park, NY: New City Press, 2007), 340.

29 Augustine of Hippo, *De Civitate Dei*, 19.13.1; 19.27.1.

30 Pope John XXIII, *Pacem in Terris* ("Encyclical Letter on Establishling Universal Peace in Truth, Justice, Charity and Liberty," April 11, 1963), no. 171, The Holy

See http://www.vatican.va/holy_father/john_xxiii/encyclicals/documents/hf_j-xxiii_enc_11041963_pacem_en.html (accessed March 10, 2014).

31 From *Our Lady of Knots: A Favorite Devotion of Pope Francis* (Huntington, IN: Our Sunday Visitor, 2013), 1.

32 Chiara Lubich, "Mary in the Focolare Movement," in *Essential Writings: Spirituality, Dialogue, Culture,* ed. Michel Vandeleene (Hyde Park, NY: New City Press, 2007), 40.

NEW CITY PRESS
of the Focolare
Hyde Park, New York

New City Press is one of more than 20 publishing houses sponsored by the Focolare, a movement founded by Chiara Lubich to help bring about the realization of Jesus' prayer: "That all may be one" (John 17:21). In view of that goal, New City Press publishes books and resources that enrich the lives of people and help all to strive toward the unity of the entire human family. We are a member of the Association of Catholic Publishers.

Further Reading—Books by New City Press

Books by Fr. Dennis J. Billy
Beauty of the Eucharist	978-1-56548-328-6	$17.95
Living in the Gap	978-1-56548-392-7	$12.95
Tending the Mustard Seed	978-1-56548-475-7	$11.95

Books by Maire O'Byrne:
Now - This Moment Matters	978-1-56548-500-6	$7.95

Periodicals
Living City Magazine,
www.livingcitymagazine.com

Scan to join our mailing list for
discounts and promotions
or go to
www.newcitypress.com
and click on "join our email list."

in their lives, a love that comes not from them, but from the Spirit of Christ living within them.

This book cannot capture the entirety of Francis' vision of the Church striving to proclaim the gospel in today's world, but it seeks to touch upon the main contours of the pope's message, which focuses on God's tenderness, love, and compassion for all human beings. Pope Francis proclaims a gospel of joy as well as a gospel of mercy, one in which the shepherds must be close to their people, love them, and carry about them "the smell of their sheep."[2]

1

Changing Focus

I prefer a Church bruised, hurting and dirty because it has been out on the streets, rather than a Church unhealthy from being confined and from clinging to its own security. I want no Church concerned with being at the center and which then ends by being caught up in a web of obsessions and procedures. If something should rightly disturb us and trouble our consciences, it is that so many of our brothers and sisters are living without the strength, light and consolation born of friendship with Jesus Christ, without a community of faith to support them, without meaning and a goal in life. More than by fear of going astray, I hope that we will be moved by the fear of remaining shut up within structures, within rules which make us harsh judges, within habits which make us feel safe, while at our door people are starving and Jesus does not tire of saying to us: "Give them something to eat" (Mk 6:37).

Evangelii Gaudium, 49

*T*hese words exemplify the change of focus that Pope Francis, in the opening months of his pontificate, has brought to the forefront of Catholic consciousness, a change that will inspire us for years to come. He does not present impossible goals that would only weary us, empty hopes that would only disappoint and weaken our resolve, added burdens that would distract us from our purpose, but a vision of the Church that asks each and every one of us take stock of the essentials of our faith and focus on what truly matters.

Pope Francis calls us back to the basics. Like Francis of Assisi, whose name he bears, he asks us to embrace the simple message of God's deep, passionate love for every human person, especially the poor and neglected. Jesus Christ embodies this love; all who call themselves Christians are his friends. Whatever we think and say and do must flow from this friendship. If it does not, our faith becomes a mockery, something other than the very faith of Jesus Christ.

A Firm Foundation

When Jesus cautioned his followers to build their houses on rock lest they be swept away by rain, wind, and flood, he was not giving architectural advice. The parable is about our spiritual life. If we don't get the basics straight, we risk losing everything. Pope Francis also challenges us to take careful stock of our situation, to step back and take a good, hard look at ourselves so we can see things more clearly and set our priorities straight. He reminds us that some aspects of faith are more important; it would be a distortion to assign greater significance to lesser truths (important as they may be). He advises us to build our lives on a firm foundation. Jesus puts it this way:

> ""Everyone then who hears these words of mine and acts on them will be like a wise man who built his house on rock. The rain fell, the floods came, and the winds blew and beat on that house, but it did not fall, because it had been founded on rock. And everyone who hears these words of mine and does not act on them will be like a foolish man who built his house on sand. The rain fell, and the floods came, and the winds blew and beat against that house, and it fell—and great was its fall!" (Mt 7:24–29)[3]

If the foundation is solid, the house will stand; if weak, it will fall. Jesus does not want us to be fools, but wise disciples. Following him is the one thing necessary. All else is secondary. If we build on him, we will experience the fullness of life. If we choose to go it alone, we must live with the consequences.

Francis asks us to avoid being distracted by secondary issues that, although worthwhile, can cause us to lose sight of life's true purpose. Christianity is not a moral cause, but a way of life centered on the person of Jesus Christ. Unless seen from the perspective of this fundamental truth of the Christian faith, all the other aspects make no sensible pattern. Francis wants us to view things properly, not focusing on smaller details but on the complete picture.

The pope's advice reflects what is often called the "hierarchy of truths" (EG 36). The Church's doctrines are not all equal; some are fundamental and therefore carry more weight than others. The dogma of the Trinity, which stands at the top of this hierarchy, is much more important than the dogma of the Virgin Birth. Similarly, even though both are solemnly defined dogmas of the faith, the Incarnation occupies a higher place in the hierarchy than does the Immaculate Conception. Because the different aspects of Catholic teaching carry different values, we can focus on what really matters because we believe and know why they matter. Although the truths may compete for our attention, we would know which of them deserves special reverence.

Gospel Living

This hierarchy of truths, the pope maintains, applies not only to doctrinal teachings but also to the Church's moral assertions (EG 37). Jesus himself has no difficulty distinguishing between the essential and the non-essential: "In everything do to others as you would have them do to you; for this is the law and the prophets" (Mt 7:12). When asked to name the greatest commandment, he replies: "'You shall love the Lord your God with all your heart, and with all your soul, and with all your mind.' This is the greatest and first commandment. And a second is like it: 'You shall love your neighbor as yourself.' On these two commandments hang all the law and the prophets" (Mt 22:37–40). Concerning the theological virtues, the apostle Paul says something similar: "For the whole law is summed up in a single commandment, 'You shall love your neighbor as yourself'" (Gal 5:14). Elsewhere, he writes: "And now faith, hope, and love abide, these three; and the greatest of these is love" (1 Cor 13:13). No matter how Christian love might be named—charity, a*gape*, the "Golden Rule" — it is synonymous with the gospel message. It deserves a place of reverence in the Church's teaching and a prominent place in our hearts.

Pope Francis puts it this way: "Works of love directed to one's neighbor are the most perfect external expression of the interior grace of the Spirit" (EG 37). Speaking of the effects of love, he points to St. Thomas' teaching that mercy is the greatest of the virtues not only because the others revolve around it, but also because it makes up for their deficiencies.[4] In the pope's mind, mercy lies at the heart of the gospel and is the *sine qua non* of Christian living (EG 37). We see how thoroughly mercy permeated Jesus' thoughts and actions in his encounter with the woman caught in adultery (Jn 8:1–11), his curing the paralytic lowered through a roof on a stretcher (Lk 5:17–32), his parable of the prodigal son (Lk 15:1–32), and his words of forgiveness from the cross (Lk 23:34) .

Those who have received mercy are called to extend it to others. Also, the pope says, the precepts of God's law should be applied with moderation (EG 38, 43). They should be considered not as threats but as guideposts that indicate the way of the Lord Jesus. The moral law lays out the way of discipleship and represents true gospel living. We embrace it not as an end but to give witness to the truth and to follow in the footsteps of Jesus, Our Lord, who said, "If any want to become my followers, let them deny themselves and take up their cross daily and follow me" (Lk 9:23).

What is Francis getting at? Christianity, he insists, is more than a list of rules and regulations. Despite the commandments' importance for Christian life, only one thing truly matters: our relationship with Jesus Christ (EG 3). If Christians focus so much on the Church's moral teachings (even basic teachings regarding the dignity of the human person and the sanctity of all human life), they may miss the joy that flows from our friendship with Christ. Francis worries that despite our good intentions, we may have misplaced our priorities. When we do so, Christianity becomes a burden rather a joy and our lives seem like an endless "Lent without Easter" (EG 6). Practicing our faith may be reduced to a list of "dos and don'ts" rather than a heartfelt living-out of our love for God manifested in observing what is good and avoiding what is evil. We are called to be joyful missionary disciples of an evangelizing community, not dour proponents of an exacting and unforgiving ecclesial institution. Francis asks us not only to change direction but also to change our hearts. If we concentrate our energies on our relationship with Jesus, everything else will fall in place.

The Smell of the Sheep

Pope Francis has said, memorably, that the evangelizing community must take on the "smell of the sheep" (EG 24). These words apply not merely to those with leadership roles such as bishops, priests, and religious, but to all members of the believing community. Jesus' followers are called to get their hands dirty, to contact the lost or marginalized. They must welcome the stranger, comfort the sick, feed the hungry, and visit those in prison (Mt 25:31–46). Jesus calls them to seek the impoverished and the needy, treating them with the dignity they deserve. They do so because Jesus did this. This was his *modus operandi*, his way of acting. He himself said, " 'Truly I tell you, just as you did it to one of the least of these who are members of my family, you did it to me' " (Mt 25: 40).

The entire gospel message is based on the premise that God seeks those who have strayed from his love. What is Christianity all about? This: God loved us so much he entered our world (in the Incarnation), gave himself to us completely to the point of dying for us (in his passion and death), to become nourishment for us (in the Eucharist) and a source of hope (in his Resurrection). Christianity must not be limited to our search for God; it is above all God's search for us. God pursues us like a shepherd seeking his lost sheep (Lk 15:1–7) or the woman who sweeps her house looking for a lost coin (Lk 15:8–10) or the father who rushes out of his house to greet his returning prodigal son (Lk 15:20). To cite Francis Thompson's poem, God is like a "hound of heaven" who pursues us "down the nights and down the days…down the arches of the years…down the labyrinthine ways."[5] He does this for no other reason than that he loves us. "God is love" (1 Jn 4:8), John's gospel says, a love that is self-diffusive, that can hardly contain itself. God pursues us because he is madly in love with us. He is "Iddio Pazzo," as St. Alphonsus de Liguori was fond of saying, "a crazy God," whose extreme love for us is revealed in what, humanly speaking, seem extreme measures.[6]

Taking on the "smell of the sheep" recalls an early Christian depiction of Jesus as the Good Shepherd returning to his flock carrying a lost lamb over his shoulders. Based on Jesus' parable of the lost sheep (Lk 15:1–7) and his description of himself as the good shepherd who lays down his life for his sheep (Jn 10:11), the image illustrates the lengths to which God secures our safety and well-being. Pope Francis notes that Christians are not merely to ponder love, but to put it into action. It is the love of the Word-made-flesh who "lived among us" (Jn 1: 14). It speaks of the love of a God who entered human life in the darkness of his mother's womb and who left it in the darkness of an empty tomb. It is a reminder that from his birth in Bethlehem to his death in Jerusalem, Jesus' earthly life was marked by a closeness to the people unprecedented in the priestly or prophetic tradition. Out of love he spoke with authority, proclaimed the imminent arrival of God's reign, demonstrating it through astonishing teachings, powerful works of healing, and dramatic expressions of compassion and forgiveness.

Francis' message is simple: Since Christ took on the smell of the sheep, so must we. He warns Christians against letting their faith become an armchair religion, as if they could live the gospel from afar, without getting involved in any of the grimy details of life, escaping its daily challenges. This warning applies to all of Christ's followers, especially to its leaders. Pope Francis cites the three major temptations the Church today must resist: that it be run like a business, that it be treated like an ideology, and that it foster clericalism and careerism.[7] He acknowledges the Church's need to clean house, to renew its structures at every level, beginning with the papacy and the curia and extending to every level of its organization (EG 27–33). Jesus said, "[W]hoever wishes to be great among you must be your servant, and whoever wishes to be first among you must be your slave; just as the Son of Man came not to be served but to serve, and to give his life a ransom for many" (Mt 20:26–28). Recognizing that "mere administration can no longer be enough," Pope Francis calls us to be "permanently in a state of mission" (EG 23).

Church institutions must serve the people of God—not vice versa. They exist not to perpetuate themselves, but to benefit God's people. The Church is not a bureaucracy, but a family. When its leaders lose sight of their purpose, when they forget what they are about and why they hold the positions they do, it is time for change. "The wind blows where it chooses" (Jn 3:8); the Spirit moves in God's good time. Pope Francis knows that the Spirit has always been with the Church and will never abandon God's family. He recognizes that the Church is called to continual conversion, a call in every generation. The word "conversion" (or *metanoia* in the Greek) means turning around, having a fundamental change of heart. This call, which lies at the heart of the pope's message, is meant for all who have ears to hear. To carry out its mission, the Church must look at its structures, examine its motives, and make adjustments for the good of God's people. Only a Church renewed — on all its levels — can help bring about a renewal of hearts in the world today.

A Transforming Presence

Renewing the human heart is a work of God. We share in this work by cooperating with it. Before his return to the Father, the Risen Lord gave the apostles a missionary mandate: "Go therefore and make disciples of all nations, baptizing them in the name of the Father and of the Son and of the Holy Spirit, and teaching them to obey everything that I have commanded you" (Mt 28:19–20). This mission touches the heart of the Church's existence and underscores its intimate relationship to Christ who, as head of the body, the Church, has promised to remain with us always "to the end of the age" (Mt 28:20).

The Church, Francis tells us, goes forth on its apostolic activity to convert and transform the world. Its transforming presence announces God's kingdom and makes it a reality through preaching (*kerygma*), fellowship *(koinonia)*, service (*diakonia*), and celebration of the sacraments (*liturgia*), all of which are actions of Christ that herald the new creation. If the Church is to transform the world, Pope Francis reminds us, its members must be converted to Christ. Our message must flow from the heart of the gospel, which has taken root in our souls.

This mission, the pope tells us, must take a human shape and so must be continually reformulated in language and expressions that are meaningful to those who hear it. He asks us to recognize the difference between the gospel itself and the forms used to express it (EG 41). As at Pentecost the disciples proclaimed the Good News in different languages, bringing about the conversion of many (Acts 2:1–13), so are we called to discover new ways to touch the hearts of those we encounter. Our mission therefore requires ongoing discernment concerning the way we preach, teach, serve, and celebrate. Also remember that our mission, which is both *ad intra* and *ad extra*, involves reaching in and reaching out. We ourselves must be evangelized to carry out our evangelizing mission.

In all of this, Pope Francis maintains, the Church remains a "mother with an open heart" (EG 46). She always leaves her door open and extends an invitation to everyone to share in her life: "Everyone can share in some way in the life of the Church; everyone can be part of the community" (EG 47). He points out that "the doors of the sacraments [must] not be closed for simply any reason" (EG 47). The Eucharist, in particular, should not be a "prize for the perfect," but "powerful medicine and nourishment for the weak" (EG 47). "[T]he confessional," moreover, "must not be a torture chamber but rather an encounter with the Lord's mercy which spurs us on to do our best" (EG 44). Also, "there is an inseparable bond between our faith and the poor" (EG 48). The Church, therefore, must go out to everyone without exception and offer them the life of Jesus Christ. The gospels indicate clearly that we should seek "not so much our friends and wealthy neighbors, but above all the poor and the sick, those who are usually despised and overlooked, 'those who cannot repay you'" (EG 48).

Conclusion

Pope Francis affirms the Church's missionary mandate to go forth and make disciples of all nations, a mandate that applies not only to clergy and religious but to every member of the faithful. As individual believers and as members of a community, evangelization requires us to abandon our complacency, to spread the Good News of Jesus Christ boldly, creatively.

To succeed in the new evangelization, we must first be evangelized ourselves. We cannot give what we ourselves do not have. Being "sacramentalized" does not mean that we have been "evangelized"; many practicing Catholics have yet to experience the joy of Christ's friendship.[8] The Church's missionary transformation must begin in our hearts and work its way outwards. It requires us to examine and rethink "the goals, structures, style and method of evangelization" (EG 33) at every level, from the Vatican to local dioceses to parishes to families, and to individuals.

Our motives must be completely transparent; we must take special care to practice what we preach. Our evangelizing efforts should energize our ordinary pastoral ministry to contact those who no longer practice their faith, even those who may have never heard the gospel message or even may have rejected it (EG 15).

The joy of the gospel is synonymous with friendship with Christ. This intimate personal relationship, which lies at the heart of the faith, changes our lives in untold ways. It is our primary means for making new disciples. When Christ's love burns in our hearts, the power of the Lord's Spirit is unleashed in our lives and wonderful things happen. Transformed by Jesus' compassion, mercy, and love we feel compelled to share it with others. Such sharing lies at the heart of our missionary mandate. When we share our experience of Christ's friendship we make disciples just as Jesus did with his earliest followers: "Come to me, all you that are weary and are carrying heavy burdens, and I will give you rest. Take my yoke upon you, and learn from me; for I am gentle and humble in heart, and you will find rest for your souls. For my yoke is easy, and my burden is light" (Mt 11:28–30). Pope Francis understands that the joy of the gospel comes from resting in the friendship and love of Christ. From this perspective, the message we proclaim is welcomed with relief because it promises great joy.

Reflection Questions

* When have you experienced the joy of Christ's friendship? How was this friendship important to you? What other forces in your life are important?

* What does Christ ask of you? How does he challenge you? How might you change focus? In what ways do you need renewal?

* In what areas does the Church need renewal? How can you participate in this work of renewal?

* What value does the work of making disciples have for you? How can you participate in the new evangelization? How can you help make disciples in your daily life?

2

Today's Challenges

The Christian ideal will always be a summons to overcome suspicion, habitual mistrust, fear of losing our privacy, all the defensive attitudes which today's world imposes on us. Many try to escape from others and take refuge in the comfort of their privacy or in a small circle of close friends, renouncing the realism of the social aspect of the gospel. For just as some people want a purely spiritual Christ, without flesh and without the cross, they also want their interpersonal relationships provided by sophisticated equipment, by screens and systems which can be turned on and off on command. Meanwhile, the gospel tells us constantly to risk a face-to-face encounter with others, with their physical presence which challenges us, with their pain and their pleas, with their joy which infects us in our close and continuous interaction. True faith in the incarnate Son of God is inseparable from self-giving, from membership in the community, from service, from reconciliation with others. The Son of God, by becoming flesh, summoned us to the revolution of tenderness.

Evangelii Gaudium, 88

The new evangelization challenges us to be active participants in a "revolution of tenderness" which, rooted in God's face-to-face encounter with us in the person of Jesus Christ, abhors violence and seeks a radical change in outlook through peaceful means. In taking on human nature in solidarity with us, God has taken on our point of view and has experienced the trials and challenges that fill our lives. By living among us, he knows intimately the temptations and suffering of being immersed in a broken world. Jesus, the Word-made-flesh, calls us to be in the world but not of it, to embrace the world, to be a leaven for it, and ultimately bring about its transformation. He wants us to be missionary disciples who, like him, follow the path of selfless giving to draw others into the sphere of divine love. We do so by fostering personal friendships through face-to-face encounters, sharing with these friends the joy of the gospel. Pope Francis refers to the "revolution of tenderness," by which we set aside the values of the world and adopt those Jesus has described in the Sermon on the Mount, in which we find the Beatitudes and even the Golden Rule (Mt 5–7).

Easier said than done. The pope understands the challenges that missionary disciples are facing at the dawn of the twenty-first century. In keeping with his formation in Ignatian spirituality, he asks us to be ever watchful of the "signs of the times" and to discern between the spirit of good and the spirit of evil. He recognizes the dehumanizing tendencies that block Christ being borne to others through evangelization (EG 51). He also believes this moment in history, marked by great technological advancement as well as growing fear and desperation, is a turning point in human experience. It is a conflict that has unsettling results: "The joy of living frequently fades, lack of respect for others and violence is on the rise, and inequality is increasingly evident. It is a struggle to live and, often, to live with precious little dignity" (EG 52). Contemporary challenges demand creative approaches which may have unorthodox or unprecedented solutions.

Present Challenges

A middle school science teacher once engaged her students in studying aerodynamics by giving them a challenge. She gave them fifteen minutes to construct a paper airplane that would travel the greatest distance, using only a single sheet of paper. Her students displayed great creativity within the allotted time and came up with a variety of designs they hoped would outdo their classmates. The winner turned out to be Jeffrey, a young boy known for unconventional behavior. He approached the line slowly, hiding something behind his back. To his teacher's and classmates' surprise he produced a plain sheet of paper. After the snickering died down, he crumpled the paper into a ball and heaved it as hard as he could. No one could match his distance. Jeffrey interpreted the challenge in a unique way and had the courage to act upon his vision.[9]

In a similar way, our journey of faith will include inevitable challenges, but we can develop our own creative responses. Jesus' disciples faced enormous challenges as they began their journeys; we should not expect otherwise. The apostle Paul writes, "We are afflicted in every way, but not crushed; perplexed, but not driven to despair; persecuted, but not forsaken; struck down, but not destroyed" (2 Cor 4:8–9). The pope asks us not to lose heart, to be creative and courageous in following the Lord, who promises not to abandon us. We need to look beyond ourselves and turn to the Lord of impossible things. St. Paul says, "I can do all things through him who strengthens me" (Phil 4:13). As we make our way through this troubled world, the pope counsels us to be "nourished by the light and strength of the Holy Spirit," and suggests how to do so (EG 50).

Pope Francis begins by focusing on the "economy of exclusion" (EG 53). He is not an economist and does not prefer one particular economic system above others; he acknowledges the Church's teaching on private property and the universal destination of goods. He is concerned about the dangerous effects of unbridled capitalism, especially the tendency in it to view human beings as consumer goods, promoting a selfish lifestyle and reinforcing indifference to the poor and marginalized. He also criticizes the "new idolatry of money" and its promotion of "the dictatorship of an impersonal economy lacking a truly human purpose" (EG 55). Such a system in which money rules rather than serves, he claims, devalues ethics, and promotes an atmosphere of self-interest in which the plight of others is disregarded (EG 57–58).

A society with such a limited worldview is marked not only by the division between "haves" and "have-nots," but also by a culture of violence (EG 59). Such a perspective promotes a superficial understanding of the human person, encourages judgment solely by appearances, relishes subjective truth, advances relativism, unleashes secularization, and ultimately contributes to unbridled individualism and the breakdown of the family (EG 61–67). Francis warns these challenges affect nearly everyone and make inculturating the faith more difficult, especially in urban centers, where people feel increasingly isolated from one another and are beset by dehumanizing influences (EG 68–75). What C. S. Lewis calls the "abolition of man"—the tendency to treat people as objects rather than subjects—becomes easy. When that happens, people become raw material to be manipulated, used, and ultimately discarded when they no longer seem useful.[10] No one would be dehumanized in this way, but the poor and marginalized are often treated like this.

Present Temptations

Pope Francis realizes these challenges affect those who provide pastoral care in the Church. Ministry is paradoxical: God uses weak human beings to carry out his work. Paul himself writes, "But we have this treasure in clay jars, so that it may be made clear that this extraordinary power belongs to God and does not come from us" (2 Cor 4:7). Elsewhere he writes: "Therefore I am content with weaknesses, insults, hardships, persecutions, and calamities for the sake of Christ; for whenever I am weak, then I am strong" (2 Cor 12:10). Francis enumerates the temptations and hardships that can prevent us from embracing our call to be "missionary disciples." He understands that "all of us are in some way affected by the present globalized culture which, while offering us values and new possibilities, can also limit, condition and ultimately harm us" (EG 77).

What might these temptations be? First, a "heightened individualism" can generate "an inordinate concern for...personal freedom and relaxation" that leads to work becoming a mere appendage to life, as if it were not an integral part of Christian identity (EG 78). The media and certain learned circles convey "a marked skepticism with regard to the Church's message, along with a certain cynicism" (EG 79). Our inner conflict can lead to an "inferiority complex" that softens Christian values and conceals Christian identity and convictions (EG 79). The resulting "vicious circle" makes us unhappy about our identity and our behavior (EG 79). Such mistrust of the Church and our own Christian identity leads to a "practical relativism." Although we may profess our beliefs publicly, our "missionary enthusiasm" weakens, causing us to act "as if God did not exist" (EG 80). We walk a tightrope between countervailing rational and irrational forces, sometimes losing our balance.

This "practical relativism" leads to other problems. We obsess about protecting our free time and consider evangelization as "a dangerous poison rather than a joyful response to God's love which summons us to mission and makes us fulfilled and productive" (EG 81). "Spiritual sloth" makes us feel discouraged and weary: "Far from a content and happy tiredness, this is a tense, burdensome, dissatisfying and, in the end, unbearable fatigue" (EG 82). Because our culture prizes immediate satisfaction, we balk at "anything that smacks of disagreement, possible failure, criticism, the cross" (EG 82). The biggest threat is "the gray pragmatism of the daily life of the Church, in which all appears to proceed normally, while in reality faith is wearing down and degenerating into small-mindedness" (EG 83). This petty "tomb psychology … slowly transforms Christians into mummies in a museum," without hope and infected by a latent melancholy that blots out our gospel joy (EG 83).

We must cast off such negativity, which turns us into the "living dead." Jesus himself says that ours is a God of the living, and not of the dead (see Mk 12: 27). Francis exhorts us to reject the spiritual pessimism and worldliness that can easily infect our minds and hearts. He encourages us to resist "a defeatism which turns us into querulous and disillusioned pessimists, 'sourpusses'" (EG 85). No one likes a grumpy disciple. The pope also bids us to cooperate with one another and to refuse the spiritual "desertification" that can affect the public square, the workplace, the family, the human heart, every area of life. In this spiritual desert, he sees a unique opportunity to discover the deep spiritual thirst and hunger of the heart by which we can "rediscover the value of what is essential for living" (EG 86). With the eyes of faith "we can see the light which the Holy Spirit always radiates in the midst of darkness" (EG 84). The Lord offered himself "as a source of living water"; "we are called to be living sources of water from which others can drink" (EG 86).

Saying "Yes" to God

Christian life can be described as a movement away from the disordered attachments of the world ("detachment") and toward the things of God or "life in the Spirit" ("union"). St. Paul puts it this way: "For those who live according to the flesh set their minds on the things of the flesh, but those who live according to the Spirit set their minds on the things of the Spirit" (Rom 8:5). Reflecting this important principle of the spiritual life, Pope Francis tells us that as missionary disciples we must say "no" to some things and "yes" to others.

Earlier in his message he says "no" to the economy of exclusion, the new idolatry of money, a financial system that rules rather than serves, and an inequality that spawns violence. He cites the challenges that make inculturating the faith in today's world difficult, challenges that affect every Christian. So we also must say "no" to selfishness, complacency, and the sterile pessimism that can make us ashamed of our faith, embrace a relativistic attitude toward life, and even turn us into practical atheists. Pope Francis calls for a "no" to the spiritual worldliness that divides our hearts that sets us against ourselves and others. Christianity is not a religion of "dos and don'ts." We say "no" to certain things not for the sake of saying "no," but because we have discovered a "pearl of great price" (Mt 13:46), which is the only thing that matters: our relationship with Jesus Christ.

The pope wants us to say "yes" to whatever will deepen our relationship with Christ. To do so, we must open our hearts in prayer, asking God to reveal himself to us. We must get down on our knees and ask for help in establishing a personal relationship with God. We must spend time in silent prayer seeking deep within our hearts the One all along seeking us. We must attend to the still, small voice within our hearts constantly whispering, "I love you. I love you. I love you." We must become one of the Lord Jesus' disciples and embrace the challenge of missionary spirituality. We must go forth and make disciples of those we encounter in our daily lives through the words we say, and the things we do. We must witness to Christ's love for us through selfless giving to everyone we meet, especially the poor and marginalized.

After saying "yes" to Christ by inviting him into our hearts and following him as missionary disciples, we must also say "yes" to his Spirit, who lights up our path and through holy promptings guides us. Saying "yes" to the Spirit means saying "yes" to relationships rooted in Christ, forged in love, and open to new life. We are called out of isolation and challenged "to overcome suspicion, habitual mistrust, fear of losing our privacy, all the defensive attitudes which today's world imposes on us" (EG 88). Rather than escaping into the comfort of a small circle of friends, turning ourselves inward and away from the social dimension of the gospel, we are called to face-to-face encounters by which we can carry to them Christ's invitation to plentiful and abundant life. If we allow God to live in our hearts and his Spirit to shape and polish us into images of divine love, we bear Christ to others. The apostle Paul describes what this entails:

> As God's chosen ones, holy and beloved, clothe yourselves with compassion, kindness, humility, meekness, and patience. Bear with one another and, if anyone has a complaint against another, forgive each other; just as the Lord has forgiven you, so you also must forgive. Above all, clothe yourselves with love, which binds everything together in perfect harmony. And let the peace of Christ rule in your hearts, to which you were called in the one body. And be thankful. Let the word of Christ dwell in you richly; teach and admonish one another in all wisdom; and with gratitude in your hearts sing psalms, hymns, and spiritual songs to God. And whatever you do, in word or deed, do everything in the name of the Lord Jesus, giving thanks to God the Father through him.
>
> Col 3:12–17

God shapes each of us into an *alter Christus* (another Christ) by entering into relationship with us and offering his friendship (Jn 15:15), which is marked by benevolence, reciprocity, and mutual indwelling.[11] Sirach says, "Faithful friends are a sturdy shelter" (Sir 6:14 NAB). True friends look out for one another and carry each other in their hearts. Being friends with Christ means he seeks our well-being and in return we seek to do his will. He dwells in our hearts and we dwell in his. As Paul eloquently attests:

"For through the law I died to the law, so that I might live to God. I have been crucified with Christ; and it is no longer I who live, but it is Christ who lives in me. And the life I now live in the flesh I live by faith in the Son of God, who loved me and gave himself for me" (Gal 2:19–21). To live in Christ means to die to sin and the works of the flesh, to be filled with his Spirit manifested by spiritual fruits: "love, joy, peace, patience, kindness, generosity, faithfulness, gentleness, and self-control" (Gal 5: 22–23). By these signs others will see we are followers of Christ. The more these fruits are manifested in our lives, the more closely are our hearts conformed to Christ, and Christ to ours.

Living in the Spirit

Disciples today face many challenges, both negative and positive. The negative ones come from the world's distractions and misdirected values that weigh us down and distract us from our goal, pulling us from our ultimate purpose in life. We become divided both within ourselves and in our relationship with others.

On the positive side, God challenges us to relinquish whatever prevents us from loving him and to cling to whatever deepens our love for him and our desire to live for others. The challenge of discipleship, its "cost," is a gradual process of conversion in which we loosen our hold onto our own lives and allow God's Spirit to take possession of us and move us along the way of holiness. Alphonsus de Liguori said that "the paradise of God is the human heart."[12] For Pope Francis, the joy of the gospel is simple: God wishes to live in our hearts. When we let God do so his Spirit dwells there, purging our imperfections and slowly divinizing us so that as free and faithful disciples we follow the way of the Lord Jesus. Being a disciple challenges us to allow our relationship with Christ to become so intimate we identify completely with him and our life becomes a continual dance, his Spirit who resides in our hearts directing and prompting us from within.

Before all else, being led by the Spirit means being committed to a life of prayer. When he was Archbishop of Buenos Aires, Jorge Mario Bergoglio wrote: "Prayer is talking and listening. There are moments of profound silence, adoration, waiting to see what will happen."[13] Prayer, he says, is the space in our lives we open up to God. We can do this: through petitions, meditation, reading Scripture, contemplation—to name a few. Since we are both individual and social by nature, it also follows that our prayer will reflect a balance between personal devotion and membership in Christ's body, the Church. "The spirit of the liturgical celebration," Archbishop Bergoglio maintained, "must be linked with the spiritual, with the encounter with God."[14] Prayer is our encounter with God; it is the air we breathe that helps us to live a life in the Spirit. We may not see the Spirit's presence in our lives if we have not sought the Lord in prayer. Any close relationship must be nurtured through spending time with each other. The same is true of our rapport with God. We nurture our relationship with him when we seek him in prayer with body, mind, and spirit. If we do not pray, we can never be on intimate terms with God. If we do not pray, we will not understand how to live a life led by the Spirit. We may know something about the Spirit, but we will never experience the Spirit working actively in our lives.

The Spirit's presence in our lives makes various gifts and fruits work in harmony to achieve a synergy within us. Aristotle observed that "The whole is greater than the sum of the parts."[15] Our "parts" operate in concert with one another, rarely in isolation. The Spirit's gifts and fruits do not call attention to themselves or even to the person upon whom they are bestowed. They exist to give God glory by transforming us more and more into his image and likeness. They may not always be active; the Spirit puts them to use as the need arises. Ultimately, gospel joy comes from our cooperation with God's free offer of abundant grace.

Conclusion

Disciples face many complex challenges: individualism, secularization, the idolatry of money, globalization, relativism, and practical atheism—to name but a few. Their inescapable influence fills our world. We may even feel overwhelmed by them. Pope Francis identifies these challenges, names them for what they are, and encourages us not to lose hope. Discipleship, he reminds us, demands courage and strength. Following Jesus means taking up the cross and walking in his footsteps. These challenges demand original thinking, that we look beyond the cross, fixing our eyes on the empty tomb and opening our hearts to the Spirit of the Risen Lord.

The earliest disciples knew what they would face. Jesus himself warned them: "If the world hates you, be aware that it hated me before it hated you... . . If they persecuted me, they will persecute you" (Jn 15:18, 20). At his command, his disciples traveled the world, took risks, and faced countless dangers with great courage These challenges did not discourage them because in the face of insurmountable odds the Spirit comforted them, strengthened their resolve, emboldened them, and confirmed them in their mission. Their love for God and the Spirit of the Lord moved these disciples to share that love with others.

Some of our challenges resemble those of the earliest disciples; others, products of our own day and age, demand new and untried responses. However they affect us—in ways large or small—Pope Francis encourages us to face them head-on with the same missionary zeal: "Challenges exist to be overcome! Let us be realists, but without losing our joy, our boldness and our hope-filled commitment. Let us not allow ourselves to be robbed of our missionary vigor!" (EG 109).

Reflection Questions

* What challenges do you face in your daily life? Where do they come from? How are you dealing with them? How do they hold you back or prevent you from following Jesus?

* Are you affected by any that Pope Francis mentions? Which affect you more than others? Which have worn you down? Which seem to diminish your joy and missionary vigor? What can you do to regain what you have lost?

* How do these challenges offer an opportunity for growth? With God all things are possible. How does knowing that help you?

3

The New Evangelization

> The Lord's missionary mandate includes a call to growth in faith: "Teach them to observe all that I have commanded you" (Mt 28:20). Hence the first proclamation also calls for ongoing formation and maturation. Evangelization aims at a process of growth which entails taking seriously each person and God's plan for his or her life. All of us need to grow in Christ. Evangelization should stimulate a desire for this growth, so that each of us can say wholeheartedly: "It is no longer I who live, but Christ who lives in me" (Gal 2:20).
>
> *Evangelii Gaudium*, 160

The Church faces the challenge of working to develop the new evangelization. These efforts are "new" not because the original proclamation was weak and ineffective, but because the gospel message must be preached anew to every generation. This proclamation, must touch people's lives and speak to their hearts. Otherwise, the gospel can lose its vigor, become stale or irrelevant, and seem more like "No News" than the "Good News" it is.

Many Christians, ourselves included, may have been "sacramentalized" but not "evangelized." I know I was (and feel I still am!). Receiving the sacraments does not make us true disciples. They are not magical incantations, but living signs and concrete invitations that deepen our relationship with Christ so we can give witness to him in our lives. To put it another way, we are called both to evangelize and be evangelized. The encounter with Jesus Christ always leads to being sent to others by Jesus Christ. Pope Francis points out that the gospel is not a mummified artifact on display in a museum, but a vibrant, living reality that motivates our hearts and minds. Jesus' mandate to make disciples of all nations applies as much to us as it did to his earliest followers. We must not ignore our mission of proclaiming God's love; we must strive to find new ways of communicating this message. Jesus said, "No one puts new wine into old wineskins; otherwise, the wine will burst the skins, and the wine is lost, and so are the skins; but one puts new wine into fresh wineskins." (Mk 2:22). The wine of the gospel is forever new. Today, as always, we must present it so it meets people where they are, speaks to their present circumstances, and calls them to a change of heart.

The Whole Church Proclaims

The Church may be on a pilgrim journey, but sometimes it seems to be traveling at a snail's pace, on crutches and with one hand tied behind its back. It doesn't seem to use its most important asset: its people. The faithful seem detached, uninvolved in carrying out the Church's mission. Pope Francis, in keeping with the teachings of the Second Vatican Council, is trying to root out some of such stubborn, deeply entrenched attitudes and direct Christ's Church onto its true path.

In the past, evangelization was misperceived to be the work of a select few. Some Catholics thought (and many still do) that only Church professionals—bishops, priests, and religious—were responsible for evangelization, while those in the pews were to concern themselves with more mundane affairs. Clergy and religious were entrusted with the Church's missionary mandate of preaching, teaching, and sanctifying, while the rest of the faithful were to keep the commandments and be faithful to their responsibilities and vocational commitments. The laity were not considered active participants in the work of the gospel, but passive onlookers to be seen and not heard, and to do what they were told.

Old habits die hard. Recently, many parents thought that the primary responsibility for educating children in the faith rested with the parish priests and the religious sisters in the parish school. The parents got their children to church on Sunday, sending them to Catholic school or religious education class, and making sure they received the sacraments. Everything else was left to those "in charge"—and "in charge" they were! Not all that long ago the pastor's decisions for the parish or the school principal's disciplinary actions were never questioned, even when they were flawed or ineffective! There are many reasons for this misconception of evangelization's nature and scope, mainly because of a two-tiered (almost dichotomized) understanding of discipleship and the Christian call to holiness. The beatitudes were the way of life for clergy and religious, but everyone else was to obey the commandments. The former were the missionaries, evangelists, and catechists; the latter, those missionized, evangelized, and catechized. The distinction was clear: some were considered "super Christians," so-to-speak, and others ordinary, "run of the mill" Christians. Families were not considered "domestic churches,"[16] but receptacles to be filled with the Church's doctrinal and moral teachings by authoritative figures.

The Second Vatican Council clarified this misunderstanding by proclaiming "the universal call to holiness," depicting the entire Church as "a pilgrim people" on a journey to God.[17] This call and journey are at the heart of what it means to be a follower of Jesus. In this respect, all Christians—priests, religious, and laity—are called to the work of evangelization. All are called to the same primary mission, to spread the gospel, and do so in and through the community of faithful. Pope Francis puts it this way: "Evangelization is the task of the Church. The Church…is a people advancing on its pilgrim way toward God. She is certainly a mystery rooted in the Trinity, yet she exists concretely in history as a people of pilgrims and evangelizers, transcending any institutional expression, however necessary" (EG 111). God's people must seek the Spirit's guidance in all things and keep their eyes fixed on their final destination. If they do not, like the ancient Hebrews in Sinai (Nm 32:13), they will lose themselves in the desert wilderness they encounter along the way. They will lose their bearings and wander aimlessly through life without sense or purpose.

The Church's purpose, its reason for being, its "mission statement," if you will, is to "make disciples of all nations" (Mt 28:19).[18] For Francis, every believer shares in this mission, since the entire people of God proclaim the message (EG 111). Although the Church, as the body of Christ, has many members, each with a particular function within the body, all are still one and work together for a single purpose. St. Paul writes, "God has so arranged the body... that there may be no dissension within the body, but the members may have the same care for one another. If one member suffers, all suffer together with it; if one member is honored, all rejoice together with it" (1 Cor 12:24–26). Similarly, in the Church the members have different roles, but all are involved in the work of evangelization and building the kingdom of God. Pope Francis clarifies this:

> In virtue of their baptism, all the members of the People of God have become missionary disciples (cf. Mt 28:19). All the baptized, whatever their position in the Church or their level of instruction in the faith, are agents of evangelization, and it would not envisage a plan of evangelization to be carried out by professionals while the rest of the faithful would be passive recipients. The new evangelization calls for personal involvement by

> each of the baptized. Every Christian is challenged, here and now, to be engaged in evangelization; anyone who has truly experienced God's saving love needs little time or lengthy training to proclaim that love. Every Christian is a missionary if he or she has encountered the love of God in Christ Jesus: we no longer say we are "disciples" and "missionaries," but rather that we are always "missionary disciples."
>
> (EG 120)

Scripture itself testifies to this truth: "If the whole body were an eye, where would the hearing be? If the whole body were hearing, where would the sense of smell be?" (1 Cor 12:17). Elsewhere it states: "Like good stewards of the manifold grace of God, serve one another with whatever gift each of you has received. Whoever speaks must do so as one speaking the very words of God; whoever serves must do so with the strength that God supplies" (1 Pt 4:10–11). Evangelization is work that Christ and his Church do together. Pope Francis reminds us of this: "It is an absurd dichotomy to love Christ without the Church; to listen to Christ but not the Church; to be with Christ at the margins of the Church. One cannot do this. It is an absurd dichotomy."[19] As missionary disciples, we are each called to roles in the Church to serve God's purpose. We must mature in the work of evangelization so we can transmit the gospel in new ways and inculturate it in today's world. The Holy Spirit working through the Church is the principal agent of this evangelization, and culture is its primary medium. As the new evangelization unfolds, we are called to be in tune with the Spirit and so we can respond to God's promptings and understand how we can bring the gospel to people of every background and culture.

Evangelization proceeds through informal preaching that begins with personal dialogue, moves on to breaking open the Word of God, and then ends with prayer (EG 127–28). It involves witnessing to people from all walks of life and on every societal level. Expressions of popular spirituality and piety such as the worldwide Marian shrines (e.g., Lourdes, Fatima, Aparecida, Guadalupe), the rosary, Forty Hours devotion, and the Divine Mercy chaplet are effective instruments of evangelization, and are seen as "a spirituality incarnated in the culture of the lowly" (EG 123–26). The pope also calls for other efforts to establish a program of creative apologetics to bring the light of faith to the frontiers of human knowledge through dialogue with scientific and other intellectual circles on university campuses, both Catholic and secular (EG 132–34). Because the different charisms within the Church and theology itself are instruments of evangelization, they cannot be bound to a desk or left resting in an armchair (EG 133). Above all, "'there can be no true evangelization without the explicit proclamation of Jesus as Lord' and without 'the primacy of the proclamation of Jesus Christ in all evangelizing work'" (EG 110).

Preaching the Word

Preachers know that "A good homily can change a person's life for the better and a bad one, for the worse." This statement recalls something St. Alphonsus de Liguori (1696–1787) said:

> It is not enough to preach...it is necessary to preach in a proper manner. First, in order to preach well learning and study are necessary. He who preaches at random will do great harm to religion. Second, an exemplary life is necessary. The sermons of a man whose conduct excites contempt shall be despised.[20]

Preaching the Good News of Jesus Christ's merciful love, through words or witness, is a primary, irreplaceable means of evangelization. Because of its central role in communicating and spreading the faith, Pope Francis devotes considerable space to its important ministerial action and responsibility within the Church. He acknowledges that homilies can make both the faithful and their ordained ministers suffer: "the laity from having to listen to them and the clergy from having to preach them!" (EG 135). Preaching the gospel, one of the Church's most important responsibilities, should not be boring and lifeless, but a dynamic and penetrating encounter with God's Word. St. Paul states, "If I proclaim the gospel, this gives me no ground for boasting, for an obligation is laid on me, and woe to me if I do not proclaim the gospel!" (1 Cor 9:16).

In its broad sense, preaching takes many forms. Alan of Lille (1116/17–1202) once remarked that it takes place through the spoken word (homilies and sermons), the written word (books and treatises), and deeds (the living witness of Christian love).[21] The pope's namesake, Francis of Assisi (1181–1226), admonished his friars, "Preach the Gospel at all times, and when necessary, use words."[22] These examples suggest that in its general sense preaching is not confined to any one medium. Spreading the gospel through art or even social media can be preaching. Despite the multitude of a ways to proclaim the message, Pope Francis emphasizes that in its deepest sense preaching concerns the proclamation of the gospel through the spoken word. After all, according to St. Paul, "Faith comes from what is heard, and what is heard comes through the word of Christ" (Rom 10:17). Nothing can replace the explicit proclamation of God's Word.

In *The Joy of the Gospel*, Pope Francis devotes considerable space to the homily. This "touchstone for judging a pastor's closeness and ability to communicate to his people" (EG 135) is "a dialogue between God and his people, a dialogue in which the great deeds of salvation are proclaimed and the demands of the covenant are continually restated" (EG 137). The homily, the pope states, also "has special importance due to its Eucharistic context: it surpasses all forms of catechesis as the supreme moment in the dialogue between God and his people which lead up to sacramental communion" (EG 137). It is not meant to be entertainment. This is "a distinctive genre", since it is preaching situated within the framework of a liturgical celebration. It should be brief and avoid appearing to be a speech or lecture (EG 138). Since preachers speak on behalf of the Church, they must address the faithful "in the same way that a mother speaks to her child, knowing that the child trusts that what she is teaching is for his or her benefit, for children know that they are loved" (EG 139).

Preachers must try to set their listeners' hearts on fire: "A preaching which would be purely moralistic or doctrinaire, or one which turns into a lecture on biblical exegesis, detracts from this heart-to-heart communication which takes place in the homily" (EG 142). They must look beyond weaknesses and failings to see listeners as Jesus sees them (EG 141). Preaching must not communicate merely ideas or detached values, but synthesize what lies within the heart: "To speak from the heart means that our hearts must not just be on fire, but also enlightened by the fullness of revelation and by the path travelled by God's word in the heart of the Church and our faithful people throughout history" (EG 144).

The pope also emphasizes the importance of preparation, offering a method for doing so. Preachers should call upon the Holy Spirit in prayer, approach the text with a deep reverence for the truth, take care to study the meaning of the text with the greatest care, focus on the text's central message, relate that message to the entire teaching of the Church, and allow it to penetrate their own thoughts and feelings so it resonates in their hearts (EG 146–50). By personalizing the message, preachers allow God's word to penetrate their entire being and keep them from proclaiming God's message in a shallow, inauthentic way. St. Augustine suggests, "For now, treat the Scripture of God as the face of God. Melt in it presence."[23] "What is essential," the pope insists, "is that the preacher be certain that God loves him, that

Jesus Christ has saved him and that his love always has the last word" (EG 151). Preachers can achieve this through *lectio divina*. This practice of spiritual reading begins with studying the text in its literal meaning and then discerning how the words speak to one's own life. (EG 152). A preacher who does not allow God's word to penetrate his heart "will indeed be a false prophet, a fraud, a shallow impostor" (EG 151).

Sometimes, Sunday homilies can go over the parishioners' heads, as if they were being preached to in a foreign language. Good preachers must speak the language of their people. Besides allowing God's word to touch and penetrate his own heart, an effective homilist "also needs to keep his ear to the people and to discover what it is that the faithful need to hear" (EG 154). Preachers must contemplate not only the word, but also the people they serve (EG 154). This twofold contemplative activity enables them to connect the biblical text with the human situation and speak in a way that brings listeners farther along the way of salvation. Preaching in this way demands spiritual sensitivity and discernment. Preachers must know their congregations' concerns and speak in a way that meets them where they are and leads them into a deeper, more authentic relationship with the Lord. They must avoid technical language and use homiletic resources in a way that respects the content of evangelization and its method. A good homily, the pope says, should have three things: "an idea, a sentiment, an image" (EG 157). It should use simple, positive language, not pointing out people's mistakes but suggesting what they can do better (EG

159). Preachers must be careful not to impose their own language and way of thinking on their audience. They must strive to speak so people understand and that resonates in their hearts.

Understanding the Kerygma

Some have said that "Christianity is not taught, but caught." This statement suggests that communicating the faith involves not only conveying doctrinal and moral teachings, but also bringing the message of Christ to others through a living witness—to give witness is to teach. A story about St. Clement Hofbauer (1751–1820) illustrates this point. After entering a tavern in Warsaw to beg money to support his refuge for homeless boys, an angry patron spat in his face. Hofbauer wiped off the spittle and said, "That was for me. Now what do you have for my boys?" Clement's humility so moved the men that they collected a large sum of silver to support the boys under his care.[24]

According to Pope Francis, a homily should help people understand their relationship with Christ by combining words with a witness of living faith. *Kerygma* is the proclamation of this living relationship. It seeks to engender doctrinal formation by encouraging people to grow in virtue by embracing the Lord's commandment to love one another as he has loved us (Jn 15:12). On our own we cannot love as Christ loved; it is a gift from God. The homily should help those who listen recognize their limitations and accept the gift of God's love that empowers them to love as he does. "All Christian formation," according to the pope, "consists of entering more deeply into the kerygma" (EG 165). The central message of the kerygma must be emphasized :

> [I]t has to express God's saving love which precedes any moral and religious obligation on our part; it should not impose the truth but appeal to freedom; it should be marked by joy, encouragement, liveliness and a harmonious balance which will not reduce preaching to a few doctrines which are at times more philosophical than evangelical.
>
> (EG 165)

True catechesis, he continues, lies in proclaiming the word. In its heart it is *kerygmatic*, focusing on God's mercy and love made manifest in the person of Jesus Christ. It is *mystagogic* because it involves "a progressive experience of formation involving the entire community and a renewed appreciation of the liturgical signs of Christian initiation" (EG 166). It attends to the "way of beauty" (*via pulchritudinis*) by encouraging the arts and by discovering new forms of beauty in cultural settings that will draw people to the true meaning of the gospel. Its moral component should be presented not as an end but as a response to the call of discipleship. Preaching should stress the positive message of the gospel: "Rather than experts in dire predictions, dour judges bent on rooting out every threat and deviation, we should appear as joyful messengers of challenging proposals, guardians of the goodness and beauty which shine forth in a life of fidelity to the Gospel" (EG 168).

As understanding of the kerygma deepens, the Church "will have to initiate everyone—priests, religious, and laity—into the 'art of accompaniment' which teaches us to remove our sandals before the sacred ground of the other" (EG 169). Spiritual accompaniment keeps believers from becoming spiritual drifters who wander away from God. It encourages them in their pilgrimage to the Father and teaches them to become proficient in the "art of listening" (EG 171). Centered and nourished by God's word, it helps them appropriate the divine mystery and continue the mission of evangelization. It helps them trust more deeply in God's word and encourages them to ponder God's self-revelation to them.

Conclusion

Pope Francis wants his readers to look forward by looking back. He calls them back to the Church's primary mission: the work of evangelization, proclaiming the Christian faith by giving witness to it. This work flows from the heart of the Church and forms a part of her sacred identity as the New Eve, the mother of redeemed humanity. Created in the image and likeness of God, this humanity mirrors God's own life, a community of love that pours itself out the threefold work of creation, redemption, and sanctification. This work manifests itself in the historical narrative of God's people and continues in the encounter between God's people and the world. The Church, a community of missionary disciples, is called to bear God's love to others. Through this community God continues "to make all things new" (Rev 21:5) by conforming humanity to the image and likeness of the Son through the power of the Spirit.

Pope Francis places the new evangelization at the forefront of the Church's awareness, asking the faithful to discover how they can contribute to it. Every believer shares in the life and mission of the Church and plays an important role in bringing Christ to others at this moment in history. The work of evangelization, the pope says, involves leading others to a personal, face-to-face encounter with Christ. That cannot happen unless those who lead have not first experienced the joy of such an intimate relationship. He points out, therefore, that Christians themselves must be evangelized anew, setting their own hearts on fire with the love of God and being filled with a longing to preach the gospel in all they think, say, and do. God is passionately in love with humankind, Pope Francis says, and asks every person to reciprocate that divine love by expressing it to others.

The new evangelization brings Christ to those who may never have heard his message or who have not allowed it to touch their hearts and penetrate their very being. It proclaims Jesus Christ within and beyond the community of faith, constantly seeking new ways of proclaiming the Good News of God's merciful love. To bring the gospel message to the world through inculturation, the faithful must travel great distances, not only physically but also mentally, spiritually, and culturally. To do this, they must take all that is good in the world, imbue it with the Spirit of Christ, and make it their own. They must tear down barriers of hatred and division and build bridges between people, and between them and God. The new evangelization is a loving and joyful proclamation that extends to anyone searching for the meaning of life and who wishes to live accordingly.

Reflection Questions

* What does the new evangelization mean to you? How does it differ from the old evangelization?

* What role are you supposed to play in it? How do you figure out what that role is? What are the methods of the new evangelization? What place does proclamation of Jesus Christ have in it? How are you a missionary disciple?

* Why must the gospel message be expressed in new ways? Why is it important that the gospel be inculturated? What practical methods of evangelization can you employ in your home, your community, your workplace?

4

Life in Communion

> The mystery of the Trinity reminds us we have been created in the image of that divine communion, and so we cannot achieve fulfillment or salvation purely by our own efforts. From the heart of the Gospel we see the profound connection between evangelization and human advancement, which must find expression and develop in every work of evangelization. Accepting the first proclamation, which invites us to receive God's love and to love him in return with the love which is his gift, brings forth in our lives and actions a primary and fundamental response: to desire, seek and protect the good of others.
>
> *Evangelii Gaudium*, 178

"*H*e called the twelve and began to send them out two by two and gave them authority over unclean spirits" (Mk 6:7). This passage makes the nature of the new evangelization clear: it is a work of Christ and his body, the Church, and therefore preeminently communal. Jesus sent his disciples out not alone, but in groups of two or three. He did so because evangelization, which flows from the heart of God is, before all else, the work of the intimate community of divine love. Jesus' mission stems from his intimate relationship with the Father and the Holy Spirit, given to the community of disciples at Pentecost, empowering the Church to spread the Good News of God's love for humanity to every corner of the earth (Acts 1:8; 2:1–13). Disciples proclaim to others that God is love in and through their mutual love—love generously given and humbly received.

Since it flows from the heart of the Trinity, the new evangelization continues God's own creative, redemptive, and sanctifying work. It builds the kingdom by forming community and caring for society. Christians evangelize the world by embracing and transforming it through the power of God's love. Love for God and neighbor are intimately bound: "[I]f we love one another, God lives in us, and his love is perfected in us" (1 Jn 4:12). It is the communitarian nature of the new evangelization that Pope Francis wishes to emphasize.

Reaching Society

To discover the original human language, a curious (yet insensitive) scholar kidnapped an infant and raised it to the age of reason in complete isolation. As he grew, the child's physical needs were provided for—food, clothing, shelter—but he could not see, touch, or communicate with any other human being.

This crude, heartless "experiment" produced a wild child of six or seven who could not relate to others and could not use language at all! The lack of human contact stunted the child's mental growth and development. This cold-hearted experiment confirms that self-identity develops through relationship with others.

Although it may be apocryphal, the story's point is clear: Human beings are social by nature and discover their identity through relationships. As the Vatican II document *Lumen Gentium* states, "God... does not make men holy and save them merely as individuals, without bond or link between one another. Rather has it pleased him to bring men together as one people, a people which acknowledges Him and serves him in holiness."[25] Therefore, spreading the gospel cannot focus solely on one's individual relationship with Christ. The gospel has personal and social dimensions. Because God is love (1 Jn 4:8) and because this message of love lies at the heart of the Good News, evangelization must seek to make that love visible and real in the lives of the people we serve. Pope Francis emphasizes this social dimension, cautioning us of the "constant risk of distorting the authentic and integral meaning of the mission of evangelization" (EG 176).

"The kerygma," the pope states, "has a clear social content" (EG177). This content is not a lesser, secondary element of the gospel message; it is central: "Our redemption has a social dimension because 'God, in Christ, redeems not only the individual person, but also the social relations existing between men'" (EG

177). As Aristotle attests, "Man is by nature a social animal."[26] Human nature is social. For us to experience the fullness of God's love, our social ties must be transformed. These ties include not only our close, interpersonal relationships among family and friends, but also the associations and social structures through which we organize ourselves. The gospel penetrates every dimension of human existence: "To believe that the Holy Spirit is at work in everyone means realizing that he seeks to penetrate every human situation and all social bonds" (EG 177).

The challenge of the new evangelization, for Pope Francis, is to recognize that the missionary nature of the Church requires us to contact others. We would be mistaken to consider this challenge "simply… an accumulation of small personal gestures to individuals in need, a kind of 'charity à la carte,' or a series of acts aimed solely at easing our conscience" (EG 180). Missionary discipleship means more than digging into our pockets or writing a check. It is even more than St. Martin of Tours cutting his cloak in two to cover a naked man in the dead of winter, or St. Francis of Assisi kissing and embracing a leper, or even Pope Francis hugging a visibly disfigured man during a weekly audience. As commendable as these acts are, the gospel of Christ asks much more: "Its mandate of charity encompasses all dimensions of existence, all individuals, all areas of community life, and all peoples. Nothing human can be alien to it" (EG 181). Evangelization must reach beyond the private sphere into "the complexities of current situations"(EG 183). It stems from God's desire that we be happy both in this life and in the next and from authentic faith that "always involves a deep desire to change the world, to transmit values, to leave this earth somehow better than we found it" (EG 180).

The pope admits that neither he nor the Church has "a monopoly on the interpretation of social realities or the proposal of solutions to contemporary problems" (EG 184). Nor does he spell out the Church's social teaching, since that information is readily available (EG 184).[27] He also recognizes that it is "up to the Christian communities to analyze with objectivity the situation which is proper to their own country" (EG 184). He wishes, however, to contribute some constructive insights concerning our present situation. To do so, he focuses on two central issues: "the inclusion of the poor in society" and "peace and social dialogue" (EG 185).

Loving the Poor

A stranger entered a village with nothing but a large black kettle and a spoon. At the center of the village square he placed his kettle on a stand, put in it a stone, filled it with water, then built a fire beneath it. When passers-by asked him what he was doing, he smiled and said, "I'm making soup!" "You can't make soup without vegetables. You need some peas and carrots," said one person. "What about some potatoes?" asked another. "What about some chicken?" offered yet another. Before long, all the villagers had provided ingredients. And all the while, the stranger did nothing but stir! In time, he had cooked up a hearty soup he shared with everyone, especially the poor and needy.

We need to encourage others to improve society according to genuine human values that conform to the mind of Christ. At the heart of the gospel is a humble God who "emptied himself, taking the form of a slave, being born in human likeness" (Phil 2:7–8). In this act of self-emptying, Jesus was poor to enrich humanity with the gift of divine life. We must seek to do the same. Pope Francis puts it this way: "Our faith in Christ, who became poor and was always close to them, is the basis of our concern for the integral development of society's most neglected members" (EG 186). As the community of disciples that bears his name, embraces his life, and seeks to follow his teachings, the Church follows Jesus' example: "Each individual Christian and every community is called to be an instrument of God for the liberation and promotion of the poor, and for enabling them to be fully a part of society" (EG 187). A lack of solidarity with the poor diminishes our relationship with God: "How does God's love abide in anyone who has the world's goods, and sees a brother or sister in need and yet refuses help?" (1 Jn 3:17).

Contacting the poor, for Pope Francis, "means working to eliminate the structural causes of poverty and to promote the integral development of the poor, as well as small daily acts of solidarity in meeting the real needs which we encounter" (EG 188). It extends beyond isolated acts of generosity to true solidarity with the poor, fostering convictions and habits that restore their dignity and serve the common good.

Putting on "the mind of Christ"(1 Cor 2:16) means embracing Jesus' preferential option for the poor and recognizing that by evangelizing them we are also evangelized (EG 198). It asks us to recognize that the planet on which we live belongs to all humanity and that all persons, wherever they live or whatever their resources, have a right to its benefits. The pope says that all are called "to hear the cry of the poor," to help them along the road to self-fulfillment (EG 190–91), even if it demands that "the more fortunate should renounce some of their rights so as to place their goods more generously at the service of others" (EG 190). We are asked to reduce our wastefulness so more resources might be used on behalf of the poor. It means working to ensure both "'a dignified sustenance' for all people" and "their 'general welfare and prosperity,'" especially by ensuring access to adequate education, health care, employment, and a just wage (EG 192), providing for their spiritual needs, and extending the Lord's invitation of mercy and forgiveness (EG 193, 200).

Pope Francis challenges us not to succumb to a "new self-centered paganism," begging us to remember the poor, which is an important measure of our faithfulness to the gospel (EG 195). God's heart has a special place for the poor, who are present throughout salvation history (EG 197). He wants the Church to exercise an option for the poor by being poor herself and working on their behalf (EG 198). The poor have much to teach us. By contemplating their faces we see the face of Christ (EG 199). The members of the Church are not to get lost in aimless and uncontrolled activism, but moved by the Holy Spirit to attend to the needs of the poor and to alleviate their suffering. Such action involves an authentic option for the poor that differs from ideology or exploiting them for personal gain. It embraces the poor, seeks to lift them out of their poverty, and to make them feel at home in the Christian community (EG 199). "Without the preferential option for the poor, 'the proclamation of the Gospel…risks being misunderstood or submerged in an ocean of words which daily engulfs us in today's society of mass communications'" (EG 199).

No one is exempt from concern for the poor: "'Spiritual conversion, the intensity of the love of God and neighbor, zeal for justice and peace, the Gospel meaning of the poor and of poverty, are required of everyone'" (EG 201). By recognizing Christ in our neighbor, especially in the poor and marginalized, we recognize Christ himself, who said: "'Truly I tell you, just as you did it to one of the least of these who are members of my family, you did it to me'" (Mt 25:40). This commitment to the poor requires us to have a concrete effect in their lives. The pope calls for renewed efforts to create a healthy world economy that preserves the common good and honors the dignity of every human person (EG 203). He calls not for temporary help for the poor, but for systematic change: "As long as the problems of the poor are not radically resolved by rejecting the absolute autonomy of markets and financial speculation and by attacking the structural causes of inequality, no solution will be found for the world's problems or, for that matter, to any problems" (EG 202). "Inequality," he says, "is the root of social ills" (EG 202). Rather than merely trusting in invisible market forces, he believes that growth in justice "requires decisions, programs, mechanisms and processes specifically geared to a better distribution of income, the creation of sources of employment and an integral promotion of the poor which goes beyond a simple welfare mentality" (EG 204). Every government shares in the responsibility for creating an environment that "ensures the economic well-being of all countries, not just of a few" (EG 206). Just what these decisions, programs, mechanisms, and processes might be he leaves for experts to discern and implement. He insists, however, that economic systems stem from a genuine concern to elevate the situation of the poor rather than using (and even exploiting) them to increase the wealth of a relative few.

Pope Francis understands that his words may offend some, even though he pronounces them with love and affection. His primary purpose is to remind us that Jesus closely identifies with the poor and those who follow Christ "are called to care for the vulnerable of the earth" (EG 209). After all, Jesus himself said, "Blessed are you who are poor, for yours is the kingdom of God" (Lk 6:20). These poor include "the homeless, the addicted, refugees, indigenous peoples, the elderly who are increasingly isolated and abandoned, and many others" (EG 210). They also include migrants, victims of human trafficking (children, prostitutes, the undocumented), women subjected to mistreatment and violence, and the unborn (EG

210–14). The pope asks us to defend the weak and defenseless and bids us to increase our efforts to preserve our environment so future generations may be able to benefit from and enjoy the fruits of the earth (EG 215). "[A]ll of us, as Christians are called to watch over and protect the fragile world in which we live, and all its peoples" (EG 216).

Dialogue for Peace

Life in communion also includes "peace and social dialogue." One of the sad paradoxes of our age of technology and instant communication is that more people have forgotten how to listen. This tendency applies not only to individuals, but also to corporate bodies like religions and nations. Rather than talking past one another without acknowledging that others are speaking, we need to set aside our personal concerns and listen to those with whom we disagree. Without communication we will not find peace, in this world or in the next. Faith comes through hearing: "Let anyone with ears to hear listen!" (Mk 4:9).

In the Sermon on the Mount Jesus says, "Blessed are the peacemakers" (Mt 5:9). Pope Francis points out that peace, a fruit of the gospel, "cannot be understood as pacification or the mere absence of violence resulting from the domination of one part of society over others" (EG 218). "True peace," he says, cannot "act as a pretext for justifying a social structure which silences or appeases the poor, so that the more affluent can placidly support their lifestyle while others have to make do as they can" (EG 218).

Nor is peace "simply the mere absence of warfare, based on a precarious balance of power"; instead, it must be "fashioned by efforts directed day after day toward the establishment of the ordered universe willed by God, with a more perfect justice among men" (EG 219). Such efforts must be well ordered and focused on outcomes.

Authentic dialogue takes place in charity, against a backdrop of silence in service to the truth. This quiet ground of conversation must be tended carefully, allowing the partners in dialogue to formulate their ideas and share them in an honest and respectful manner. Chiara Lubich, the founder of the Focolare Movement, puts it this way:

> Dialogue means that people meet together and even though they have different ideas, they speak with serenity and sincere love toward the other person to find some kind of agreement that can clarify misunderstandings, calm disputes, resolve conflicts, and even eliminate hatred. This dialogue, especially among the faithful of different religions, today is more indispensable than ever if we want to avoid the great evils threatening our societies.[28]

To this same end the pope offers four basic principles for promoting a dialogue for peace: (1) "Time is greater than space." (2) "Unity prevails over conflict." (3) "Realities are more important than ideas." And (4) "The whole is greater than the part" (EG 222–37). "Peace," St. Augustine says, "is the tranquility of order," which begins in this life and reaches its fulfillment in the world to come.[29] These four principles, the pope asserts, "can guide the development of life in society and the building of a people where differences are harmonized within a shared pursuit" (EG 221). When implemented they can bring about authentic and true "tranquility of order," for which everyone yearns.

Each of these principles contributes something unique to building peace. The first asks us "to work slowly but surely, without being obsessed with immediate results" so we can be more "concerned about initiating processes rather than possessing spaces" (EG 223). The second invites us "to build communion amid disagreement," to recognize that "unity is greater than conflict," and to strive for "the building of friendship in society" (EG 228). The third reminds us that ideas must not mask or be disconnected from reality, but be rooted in it to serve and improve it (EG 231–32). The fourth asserts that to avoid banality and narrowness of mind, we need to consider the entire picture (EG 234). Doing so helps us respect the whole and the parts, gives us a healthy respect for local and global events, and allows us to see the connections between them.

According to the pope, by using these four principles we can work patiently toward the new evangelization. It can be established by inculturating the gospel in concrete, practical ways that unify the nations of the earth through gospel love. They establish a context for constructive dialogue that leads to peace. They embody what Pope St. John XXIII yearned for in *Pacem in Terris* and sought to establish through the Second Vatican Council:

> Let us pray with all fervor for this peace which our divine Redeemer came to bring us. May He banish from the souls of men whatever might endanger peace. May He transform all men into witnesses of truth, justice and brotherly love. May He illumine with His light the minds of rulers, so that, besides caring for the proper material welfare of their peoples, they may also guarantee them the fairest gift of peace.[30]

Pope Francis outlines a program of dialogue by which the new evangelization can promote human development for the sake of peace and the common good. This program proposes active participation, patient listening, and mutual exchange of ideas on a variety of levels: "dialogue with states, dialogue with society—including dialogue with cultures and the sciences—and dialogue with other believers who are not part of the Catholic Church" (EG 238). As it seeks to cooperate with these various groups to promote the universal good of society, the Church offers to the discussion the light of faith and a wealth of experience.

Since Jesus Christ is peace itself (Eph 2:14), "the new evangelization calls on every baptized person to be a peacemaker and a credible witness to a reconciled life" (EG 239). The Church, according to the pope, must work with local, national, and international governments "to safeguard and promote the common good of society" (EG 239). Although the Church may not have concrete solutions for particular issues, the Christian community defends the dignity of the human person and promotes the common good in the various sectors of society (EG 241). Concerning a topic related to the common good, the relationship between faith and science, the pope calls for the new evangelization to maintain an open dialogue: "Faith is not fearful of reason; on the contrary, it seeks and trusts reason, since 'the light of reason and the light of faith both come from God' and cannot contradict each other" (EG 242).

The new evangelization also includes the Church's dialogue with other Christian communities, Jews, Muslims, Hindus, Buddhists, people of other faiths, those not associated with any religious faith tradition, atheists, and all seekers of truth (EG 250–54). In a "dialogue of charity" with such groups, religious and non-religious alike, the Church must speak the truth with tenderness and love. In these conversations, the faithful must condemn violence as way of resolving conflict, avoid any facile syncretism, expose all narrow rationalism, confront the dictatorship of relativism, warn against purely individual religious experiences, and promote authentic religious freedom (EG 255–58). In doing so, we must listen and respond, speaking with respect for the dignity of the other's point of view and a sincere desire for the good of society.

Conclusion

According to Pope Francis, because the gospel embraces every reality it must extend beyond the personal to every dimension of human society. The implications of Jesus' message, "Go into all the world and proclaim the good news to the whole creation"

(Mk 16:15) extend beyond mere geography. The gospel must be proclaimed not only to the four corners of the earth, but also to every dimension of human existence itself, including the societal. The challenge of the new evangelization is to bring the message of Christ to society by promoting peace and social justice among all of humanity through dialogue with various social entities (e.g., the state, scientific institutions, other religious traditions).

Pope Francis outlines two key areas where the new evangelization must engage human society: "including the poor in society" and "working for peace and social dialogue." As followers of Jesus, we are called to imitate him by making a preferential option for the poor and promoting their full development. We do this not by sporadic acts of charity to ease our consciences, but by working to change the structures of social injustice that prevent the poor from rising above their poverty and taking their rightful place in society. For this to happen, the world's economic structures must be changed to promote equality rather than subjugation of the many to a select few. Even though he does not pretend to propose concrete solutions to complex societal and economic issues, the pope realizes that many will resist his challenge. Nor is he willing to embrace simplistic solutions such as a welfare state that perpetuates rather than alleviates the troubled lot of the poor. Although he understands there will always be poor among us (Mk 14:7), he issues this challenge out of love and affection for all humanity, reminding us that all true followers of Christ love the poor and have their best interests at heart.

These interests are best advanced through dialogue with those who hold positions of power and those who take perspectives that differ from those of Christ and his Church. Through conversation with various state, scientific, and religious groups, the pope believes the new evangelization can build bonds of friendship that will promote social justice and the universal good. Besides dialogue, he offers four principles that can help the Church promote unity patiently, realistically, and without conflict. Although the kingdom of God lies beyond this life, the pope insists that it is being built in the here-and-now. He preaches peace, justice, and unity; he asks all believers, and all people of good will, to take it to heart.

Reflection Questions

* Why must the gospel be oriented toward society and not merely toward the individual? What does this orientation say about God's love?

* What do you consider to be the gospel?

* What is your relationship with the poor? How do you regard them? Why is the preferential option for the poor so important for the new evangelization? What concrete steps can you take in your daily life to contact the poor and marginalized?

* Why is no one exempt from promoting peace and social justice in society? What concrete steps can you take to advance peace and justice in your community?

Conclusion

A Work of the Spirit

Spirit-filled evangelizers means evangelizers fearlessly open to the working of the Holy Spirit. At Pentecost, the Spirit made the apostles go forth from themselves and turned them into heralds of God's wondrous deeds, capable of speaking to each person in his or her own language. The Holy Spirit also grants the courage to proclaim the newness of the Gospel with boldness (*parrhesía*) in every time and place, even when it meets with opposition. Let us call upon him today, firmly rooted in prayer, for without prayer all our activity risks being fruitless and our message empty. Jesus wants evangelizers who proclaim the good news not only with words, but above all by a life transfigured by God's presence.

Evangelii Gaudium, 259

*T*he Holy Spirit is the author of the new evangelization and Mary is its mother. Together, they inspire the Church and all the faithful to be courageous,

Spirit-filled missionary disciples. The Spirit is the bond of love between the Father and the Son; Mary, the faithful disciple who followed the Lord from the beginning to the end of his earthly life—and into eternity. We followers of Christ are all called to do our part in the work of the new evangelization, rooted in the Spirit, indebted to Mary Our Mother, and focused on the mission Jesus has laid before us.

Jesus clarified the Church's mission: "Go, therefore, and make disciples of all nations" (Mt 28:19). This mandate touches the heart of the Church; Jesus' own mission shapes the Church's identity. From the beginning Christians have spread the Good News of Jesus' triumph over death. As we enter the third millennium, we follow them in embracing the gospel with every fiber of our being and preaching it to the ends of the earth.

Filled with the Spirit

Pope Francis envisions a new era of evangelization, a time when all Church members will be open to the working of the Holy Spirit, and will boldly proclaim the Good News of Jesus Christ to the world. For this to happen, we must be firmly rooted in prayer, "for without [it] all our activity risks being fruitless and our message empty" (EG 259). He ends his commentary on the new evangelization reflecting on its underlying spirit (EG 260), imploring the Holy Spirit "to come and renew the Church, to stir and impel her to go forth boldly to evangelize all peoples" (EG 261).

Francis insists that all Christians are called to be "Spirit-filled evangelizers," our missionary outreach fueled by our personal encounter with Jesus (EG 262). We must deepen our relationship with the Lord and contact others in a spirit of generosity and service. A renewed missionary impulse can take shape within the Church if we quiet ourselves to hear the promptings of the Spirit in our lives and respond by working in concrete and practical ways. Francis sees this impulse being carried out in the Church and welcomes its continued growth: "The Church urgently needs the deep breath of prayer, and to my great joy groups devoted to prayer and intercession, the prayerful reading of God's word and the perpetual adoration of the Eucharist are growing at every level of ecclesial life" (EG 195). He asks us to reject false spirituality, especially forms overly privatized and which focus too much on the individual. Because every period of human history has presented challenges to missionary efforts, he urges we learn from the saints, emulating them in ways suitable for our own day (EG 263).

Like the saints, we evangelize because we love Jesus. This love enkindles our desire to share it with others: "If we do not feel an intense desire to share this love, we need to pray insistently that he will once more touch our hearts" (EG 264). We need to recover a contemplative spirit that ponders the gospel and allows it to touch our hearts. Remember that we were created for the gospel and that it responds to our deepest needs, offering us "friendship with Jesus and love for our brothers and sisters" (EG 265). Each person we meet already has "an expectation, even if an unconscious one, of knowing the truth about God, about man, and about how we are to be set free from sin and death" (EG 265). Our enthusiasm for evangelization must be rooted in this conviction and "sustained by our own constantly renewed experience of savoring Christ's friendship and message" (EG 266). As missionary disciples, we must never stop walking with Jesus in this way: "A person who is not convinced, enthusiastic, certain and in love, will convince nobody" (EG 266). As his disciples, we must live in union with Jesus as "we seek what he seeks and love what he loves" (EG 267). We must remain close to his heart, just as he remains close to his Father's heart.

Our love for Jesus manifests itself in our love and concern for his people. "Mission," the pope says, "is at once a passion for Jesus and a passion for his people" (EG 268). One passion serves the other: "Jesus is the model of this method of evangelization which brings us to the very heart of his people" (EG 269). Our closeness to him kindles in us a desire to be close to his people. Jesus' death on the cross was the culmination of a life lived totally for others, and we are called to follow. He wants us to engage with others, to enter into the reality of their lives in a kind and gentle manner. He calls us "to touch human misery, to touch the suffering flesh of others" (EG 270). Our own happiness lies in seeking the good of others and desiring happiness for them (EG 272). Every person is an object of God's infinite tenderness and worthy of love and respect (EG 274).

"Jesus truly lives," the pope says. If we believed this, we would set aside the destructive attitudes which tell us that nothing will ever change and focus instead on the reality of Jesus' triumph over sin and death (EG 275). We would find in the Risen and Glorified Lord everything we believed in, hoped for, and acted upon. We would believe "that he truly loves us, that he is alive, that he is mysteriously capable of intervening, that he does not abandon us and that he brings good out of evil by his power and his infinite creativity" (EG 278). Also, we would believe that he acts in and through us by the power of his Spirit, who frees us for mission, who "works as he wills, when he wills and where he wills" (EG 280). We would also appreciate more the power of intercessory prayer, which is not "a diversion from true contemplation" (EG 281), but "a 'leaven' in the heart of the Trinity" (EG 283) and a powerful instrument of evangelization (EG 281).

Turning to Mary

Pope Francis has a special devotion to Mary as "Our Lady, Undoer of Knots." For him, Mary "is the Mother who patiently and lovingly brings us to God, so that he can untangle the knots of our soul."[31] This devotion is especially appropriate for the missionary disciples of the new evangelization. To evangelize the world we ourselves must first be evangelized. Only if we first humbly ask the Lord to untie the tangled knots of our own souls will we be able to help untie the myriad entanglements in which the world finds itself. Once we are freed from our own restraints we can help others untie the knots within their souls.

As he concludes his reflection on the new evangelization, Pope Francis calls upon Mary and entrusts the Church to her care and protection. He tells us that Jesus gave the Church the gift of his mother when he entrusted her to the beloved disciple (Jn 19:26–27). He highlights the close relationship between Mary and the Church; just as she gave birth to the Son of God, so are we called to bear him both within our hearts and in the love we extend to others.

Mary shares our history and represents the fulfillment of our deepest dreams and hopes. She embodies "a Marian 'style' to the Church's work of evangelization" (EG 288). She was with the disciples as they waited for the Holy Spirit (Acts 1:14) and made possible the Church's first missionary efforts: "She is the Mother of the Church which evangelizes, and without her we could never truly understand the spirit of the new evangelization" (EG 284). Chiara Lubich explains what she and her companions came to understand about Mary's style of evangelization, how she so nourished herself on scripture that her every word and action transmitted Christ:

> She [Mary], set as a rare and unique creature within the Holy Trinity, was all Word of God, all dressed in the Word of God. And so strong was our impression of this understanding that it seemed to us that only angels could utter something of her.
>
> If, in fact, the Word is the splendor of the Father, Mary, so imbued with the Word of God,

> appeared to us as having incomparable beauty.
>
> And it is the Magnificat that tells us how Mary is all Word of God, as it is a continuous succession of words from scripture: the Virgin Mary was so nourished by the scriptures that in her speaking she was accustomed to use its very same expressions.
>
> And it appeared so clear to us that what characterized Mary, though in her unique perfection, should characterize every Christian: to repeat Christ, the Truth, with the personality given to each by God.[32]

Mary reveals "the revolutionary nature of love and tenderness" (EG 288). She "is able to recognize the traces of God's Spirit in events great and small. She constantly contemplates the mystery of God in our world, in human history and in our daily lives. She is the woman of prayer and work in Nazareth, and she is also Our Lady of Help, who sets out from her town with haste (Lk 1:39) to be of service to others" (EG 288). She is the model of a Spirit-filled disciple. She, the first to experience the fullness of God's redemptive love, is the star of the new evangelization. We turn to her as we seek to open this new chapter in the Church's evangelizing efforts. We look to her as the "Mother of the living Gospel" (EG 288) and ask her to be with us and to help us as we contact others and draw them closer to her Son.

Notes

1 Pope Francis, *Evangelium Gaudium* ("Apostolic Exhortation on the Proclamation of the Gospel in Today's World," November 24, 2013), The Holy See, http://www.vatican.va/holy_father/francesco/apost_exhortations/documents/papa-francesco_esortazione-ap_20131124_evangelii-gaudium_en.html (accessed March 10, 2014). Referred throughout the text as EG.

2 Pope Francis, "Homily for Holy Thursday" (March 13, 2013), The Holy See, http://www.vatican.va/ holy_father/francesco/homilies/2013/documents/papa-francesco_20130328_messa-crismale_en.html (accessed March 10, 2014).

3 Unless noted otherwise, Scripture quotations come from The *New Revised Standard Version* (National Council of the Churches of Christ, 1989).

4 Thomas Aquinas, *Summa theologiae*, II-II, q. 30, a. 4

5 Francis Thompson, "The Hound of Heaven," in *The Liturgy of the Hours*, vol. 4 (New York: Catholic Book Publishing Co., 1975), 2002–6.

6 See Frederick Jones, ed., *Alphonsus de Liguori: Selected Writings, The Classics of Western Spirituality* (New York/Mahwah, NJ: Paulist Press, 1999), 268.

7 See Thomas Reese, "Pope Francis and the Three Temptations of the Church," *National Catholic Reporter* (August 13, 2013), http://ncronline.org/news/spirituality/pope-francis-and-three-temptations-church (accessed March 10, 2014).

8 See Sherry A. Weddell, *Forming Intentional Disciples: The Path to Knowing and Following Jesus* (Huntington, IN: Our Sunday Visitor, 2012), 46.

9 See "I Dare Ya," in *Lessons in Motivation & Inspiration from MJD* (Thursday, May 29, 2008), http://coach-

mjd.blogspot.com//2008/06/i-dare-ya.html (accessed March 10, 2014).

10 C.S. Lewis, *The Abolition of Man* (New York: Macmillan, 1947), 88.

11 See Paul Wadell, *Friendship and the Moral Life* (Notre Dame, IN: University of Notre Dame Press, 1988), 130–41.

12 Alphonsus de Liguori, *The Way of Salvation and Perfection* in *The Complete Ascetical Works of St. Alphonsus de Liguori*, ed. Eugene Grimm, vol. 2 (Brooklyn, St. Louis, Toronto: Redemptorist Fathers, 1926), 395.

13 Jorge Mario Bergoglio and Abraham Skorka, *On Heaven and Earth: Pope Francis on Faith, Family, and the Church in the Twenty-First Century*, trans. Alejandro Bermudez and Howard Goodman (New York: Image, 2013), 55.

14 Ibid., 58.

15 Aristotle, *Metaphysics*, 2.

16 See the Second Vatican Council, *Lumen Gentium*, ("The Dogmatic Constitution on the Church," November 21, 1964), no. 11, The Holy See, http://www.vatican.va/archive/hist_councils/ii_vatican_council/ documents/vat-ii const 19641121_lumen-gentium_en.html (accessed March 10, 2014).

17 Ibid., nos. 39, 48,

18 See Michael White and Tom Corcoran, *Rebuilt: Awakening the Faithful, Reaching the Lost, and Making Church Matter* (Notre Dame, IN: Ave Maria Press, 2013), 38–39.

19 Pope Francis, "Daily Homily for January 30, 2014." Cited in *Aleteia*, http://www.aleteia.org/ en/religion/aggregated-content/a-christian-without-the-church-is-an-absurd-dichotomy-says-pope-5879481193463808?utm_campaign=NL_en&utm_

source=daily_newsletter&utm_medium=mail&utm_content=NL_en-31/01/2014 (accessed March 10 2014).

20 Alphonsus de Liguori, *Dignity and Duties of the Priest or Selva*, in *The Complete Works of St. Alphonsus de Liguori*, ed. Eugene Grimm, vol. 12 (Brooklyn/St. Louis/Toronto: Redemptorist Fathers, 1927), 266.

21 Alan of Lille, *The Art of Preaching*, trans. Gillian R. Evans, Cistercian Studies Series no. 23 (Kalamazoo, MI: Cistercian Publications, 1981), 20.

22 Attributed to Francis of Assisi, http://www.goodreads.com/quotes/7763-preach-the-gospel-at-all-times-and-when-necessary-use (accessed March 10, 2014).

23 Augustine of Hippo, Sermon 22.7 in *The Works of St. Augustine: Sermons*, trans. Edward Hill, vol. 1 (New York, 1990), 41–48. See also Robert Louis Wilken, *The Spirit of Early Christian Thought* (New Haven/London: Yale University Press, 2003), 50.

24 See "The Redemptorists: Saint Clement Hofbauer," http://www.cssr.com/english/saints blessed/ sthofbauer.shtml (accessed March 10, 2014).

25 Second Vatican Council, *Lumen Gentium*, no. 9

26 Aristotle, *Politics*, Bk. 1, sect. 1253a.

27 See, for example, The Pontifical Council of Justice and Peace, *The Compendium of the Social Doctrine of the Church* (June 29, 2004), The Holy See, http://www.vatican.va/roman_curia/pontifical_councils/justpeace/documents/rc_pc_justpeace_doc_20060526_compendio-dott-soc_en.html (accessed March 10, 2014).

28 Chiara Lubich, "360° Dialogue," in *Essential Writings: Spirituality, Dialogue, Culture*, ed. Michel Vandeleene (Hyde Park, NY: New City Press, 2007), 340.

29 Augustine of Hippo, *De Civitate Dei*, 19.13.1; 19.27.1.

30 Pope John XXIII, *Pacem in Terris* ("Encyclical Letter on Establishling Universal Peace in Truth, Justice, Charity and Liberty," April 11, 1963), no. 171, The Holy

See http://www.vatican.va/holy_father/john_xxiii/encyclicals/documents/hf_j-xxiii_enc_11041963_pacem_en.html (accessed March 10, 2014).

31 From *Our Lady of Knots: A Favorite Devotion of Pope Francis* (Huntington, IN: Our Sunday Visitor, 2013), 1.

32 Chiara Lubich, "Mary in the Focolare Movement," in *Essential Writings: Spirituality, Dialogue, Culture*, ed. Michel Vandeleene (Hyde Park, NY: New City Press, 2007), 40.

NEW CITY PRESS
of the Focolare
Hyde Park, New York

New City Press is one of more than 20 publishing houses sponsored by the Focolare, a movement founded by Chiara Lubich to help bring about the realization of Jesus' prayer: "That all may be one" (John 17:21). In view of that goal, New City Press publishes books and resources that enrich the lives of people and help all to strive toward the unity of the entire human family. We are a member of the Association of Catholic Publishers.

Further Reading—Books by New City Press

Books by Fr. Dennis J. Billy
Beauty of the Eucharist	978-1-56548-328-6	$17.95
Living in the Gap	978-1-56548-392-7	$12.95
Tending the Mustard Seed	978-1-56548-475-7	$11.95

Books by Maire O'Byrne:
Now - This Moment Matters	978-1-56548-500-6	$7.95

Periodicals
Living City Magazine,
www.livingcitymagazine.com

Scan to join our mailing list for
discounts and promotions
or go to
www.newcitypress.com
and click on "join our email list."